THE PROTESTANT WORK ETHIC AND THE SPIRIT OF CAPITALISM

Max Weber

VIGEO PRESS

Public Domain
Translated by Talcott Parsons
Charles Scribner's Sons: New York, 1930.

Vigeo Press Reprint, 2017

ISBN
    Paperback 978-1-941129-70-8

CONTENTS

INTRODUCTION

A product of modern European civilization, study-
ing any problem of universal history, is bound to ask
him- self to what combination of circumstances the fact
should be attributed that in Western civilization, and in
Western civilization only, cultural phenomena have appeared which (as we like to think) lie in a line of development having *universal* significance and value.

Only in the West does science exist at a stage of development which we recognize today as valid. Empirical
knowledge, reflection on problems of the cosmos and of
life, philosophical and theological wisdom of the most
profound sort, are not confined to it, though in the case
of the last the full development of a systematic theology
must be credited to Christianity under the influence of
Hellenism, since there were only fragments in Islam and
in a few Indian sects. In short, knowledge and observation of great refinement have existed elsewhere, above
all in India, China, Babylonia, Egypt. But in Babylonia
and elsewhere astronomy lacked—which makes its development all the more astounding—the mathematical
foundation which it first received from the Greeks. The
Indian geometry had no rational proof; that was another product of the Greek intellect, also the creator of mechanics and physics. The Indian natural sciences, though
well developed in observation, lacked the method of experiment, which was, apart from beginnings in antiquity, essentially a product of the Renaissance, as was the
modern laboratory. Hence medicine, especially in India,
though highly developed in empirical technique, lacked
a biological and particularly a biochemical foundation.
A rational chemistry has been absent from all areas of
culture except the West.

1

The highly developed historical scholarship of China did not have the method of Thucydides. Machiavelli, it is true, had predecessors in India; but all Indian political thought was lacking in a systematic method comparable to that of Aristotle, and, indeed, in the possession of rational concepts. Not all the anticipations in India (School of Mimamsa), nor the extensive codification especially in the Near East, nor all the Indian and other books of law, had the strictly systematic forms of thought, so essential to a rational jurisprudence, of the Roman law and of the Western law under its influence. A structure like the canon law is known only to the West.

A similar statement is true of art. The musical ear of other peoples has probably been even more sensitively developed than our own, certainly not less so. Polyphonic music of various kinds has been widely distributed over the earth. The cooperation of a number of instruments and also the singing of parts have existed elsewhere. All our rational tone intervals have been known and calculated. But rational harmonious music, both counterpoint and harmony, formation of the tone material on the basis of three triads with the harmonic third; our chromatics and enharmonics, not interpreted in terms of space, but, since the Renaissance, of harmony; our orchestra, with its string quartet as a nucleus, and the organization of ensembles of wind instruments; our bass accompaniment; our system of notation, which has made possible the composition and production of modem musical works, and thus their very survival; our sonatas, symphonies, operas; and finally, as means to all these, our fundamental instruments, the organ, piano, violin, etc.; all these things are known only in the Occident, although programme music, tone poetry, alteration of tones and chromatics, have existed in various musical traditions as means of expression.

In architecture, pointed arches have been used elsewhere as a means of decoration, in antiquity and in Asia; presumably the combination of pointed arch and cross-arched vault was not unknown in the Orient. But the rational use of the Gothic vault as a means of distributing

pressure and of roofing spaces of all forms, and above all
as the constructive principle of great monumental buildings and the foundation of a *style* extending to sculpture
and painting, such as that created by our Middle Ages,
does not occur elsewhere. The technical basis of our architecture came from the Orient. But the Orient lacked
that solution of the problem of the dome and that type
of classic rationalization of all art—in painting by the rational utilization of lines and spatial perspective—which
the Renaissance created for us. There was printing in
China. But a printed literature, designed only for print
and *only* possible through it, and, above all, the Press
and periodicals, have appeared only in the Occident.
Institutions of higher education of all possible types,
even some superficially similar to our universities, or at
least academies, have existed (China, Islam). But a rational, systematic, and specialized pursuit of science, with
trained and specialized personnel, has only existed in the
West in a sense at all approaching its present dominant
place in our culture. Above all is this true of the trained
official, the pillar of both the modern State and of the
economic life of the West. He forms a type of which there
have heretofore only been suggestions, which have never remotely approached its present importance for the
social order. Of course the official, even the specialized
official, is a very old constituent of the most various societies. But no country and no age has ever experienced,
in the same sense as the modern Occident, the absolute
and complete dependence of its whole existence, of the
political, technical, and economic conditions of its life,
on a specially trained *organization* of officials. The most
important functions of the everyday life of society have
come to be in the hands of technically, commercially,
and above all legally trained government officials.

Organization of political and social groups in feudal
classes has been common. But even the feudal state of
rex et regnum in the Western sense has only been known
to our culture. Even more are parliaments of periodically elected representatives, with government by dem-
agogues and party leaders as ministers responsible to

the parliaments, peculiar to us, although there have, of course, been parties, in the sense of organizations for exerting influence and gaining control of political power, all over the world. In fact, the State itself, in the sense of a political association with a rational, written constitution, rationally ordained law, and an administration bound to rational rules or laws, administered by trained officials, is known, in this combination of characteristics, only in the Occident, despite all other approaches to it.

And the same is true of the most fateful force in our modern life, capitalism. The impulse to arquisition, pursuit of gain, of money, of the, greatest possible amount of money has in itself nothing to do with capitalism. This impulse exists and has existed among waiters, physicians, coachmen, artists, prostitutes, dishonest officials, soldiers, nobles, crusaders, gamblers, and beggars. One may say that it has been common to all sorts and conditions of men at all times and in all countries of the earth, wherever the objective possibility of it is or has been given. It should be taught in the kindergarten of cultural history that this naïve idea of capitalism must be given up once and for all. Unlimited greed for gain is not in the least identical with capitalism, and is still less its spirit. Capitalism *may* even be identical with the restraint, or at least a rational tempering, of this irrational impulse. But capitalism is identical with the pursuit of profit, and forever *renewed* profit, by means of continuous, rational, capitalistic enterprise. For it must be so: in a wholly capitalistic order of society, an individual capitalistic enterprise which did not take advantage of its opportunities for profit-making would be doomed to extinction.

Let us now define our terms somewhat more carefully than is generally done. We will define a capitalistic economic action as one which rests on the expectation of profit by the utilization of opportunities for exchange, that is on (formally) peaceful chances of profit. Acquisition by force (formally and actually) follows its own particular laws, and it is not expedient, however little one can forbid this, to place it in the same category with action which is, in the last analysis, oriented to profits from exchange. Where capitalistic acquisition is rationally pursued, the corresponding action is adjusted to calculations in terms of capital. This means that the action is adapted to a systematic utilization of goods or personal services as means of acquisition in such a way that, at the close of a business period, the balance of the enterprise in money assets (or, in the case of a continuous enterprise, the periodically estimated money value of assets) exceeds the capital, i.e. the estimated value of the material means of production used for acquisition in exchange. It makes no difference whether it involves a quantity of goods entrusted *in natura* to a travelling merchant, the proceeds of which may consist in other goods *in natura* acquired by trade, or whether it involves a manufacturing enterprise, the assets of which consist of buildings, machinery, cash, raw materials, partly and wholly manufactured goods, which are balanced against liabilities. The important fact is always that a calculation of capital in terms of money is made, whether by modern book-keeping methods or in any other way, however primitive and crude. Everything is done in terms of balances: at the beginning of the enterprise an initial balance, before every individual decision a calculation to ascertain its probable profitableness, and at the end a final balance to ascertain how much profit has been made. For instance, the initial balances of a *commenda* transaction would determine an agreed money value of the assets put into it (so far as they were not in money form already), and a final balance would form the estimate on which to base the distribution of profit and loss at the end. So far as the transactions are rational, calculation underlies every single action of the partners. That a really accurate calculation or estimate may not exist, that the procedure is pure guess-work, or simply traditional and conventional, happens even today in every form of capitalistic enterprise where the circumstances do not demand strict accuracy. But these are points affecting only the degree of rationality of capitalistic acquisition.

For the purpose of this conception all that matters is that an actual adaptation of economic action to a comparison of money income with money expenses takes place, no matter how primitive the form. Now in this sense capitalism and capitalistic enterprises, even with a considerable rationalization of capitalistic calculation, have existed in all civilized countries of the earth, so far as economic documents permit us to judge. In China, India, Babylon, Egypt, Mediterranean antiquity, and the Middle Ages, as well as in modern times. These were not merely isolated ventures, but economic enterprises which were entirely dependent on the continual renewal of capitalistic undertakings, and even continuous operations. However, trade especially was for a long time not continuous like our own, but consisted essentially in a series of individual undertakings. Only gradually did the activities of even the large merchants acquire an inner cohesion (with branch organizations, etc.). In any case, the capitalistic enterprise and the capitalistic entrepreneur, not only as occasional but as regular entrepreneurs, are very old and were very widespread.

Now, however, the Occident has developed capital- ism both to a quantitative extent, and (carrying this quantitative development) in types, forms, and directions which have never existed elsewhere. All over the world there have been merchants, wholesale and retail, local and engaged in foreign trade. Loans of all kinds have been made, and there have been banks with the most various functions, at least comparable to ours of, say, the sixteenth century. Sea loans, *commenda,* and transactions and associations similar to the *Kommanditgesellschaft,* have all been widespread, even as continuous businesses. Whenever money finances of public bodies have existed, money-lenders have appeared, as in Babylon, Hellas, India, China, Rome. They have financed wars and piracy, contracts and building operations of all sorts. In overseas policy they have functioned as colonial entrepreneurs, as planters with slaves, or directly or indirectly forced labour, and have farmed domains, offices, and, above all, taxes. They have financed party leaders in elections and *condottieri* in civil wars. And, finally, they have been speculators in chances for pecuniary gain of all kinds. This kind of entrepreneur, the capitalistic adventurer, has existed everywhere. With the exception of trade and credit and banking transactions, their activities' were predominantly of an irrational and speculative character, or directed to acquisition by force, above all the acquisition of booty, whether directly in war or in the form of continuous fiscal booty by exploitation of subjects.

The capitalism of promoters, large-scale speculators, concession hunters, and much modern financial capital- ism even in peace time, but, above all, the capitalism especially concerned with exploiting wars, bears this stamp even in modern Western countries, and some, but only some, parts of large-scale international trade are closely related to it, today as always.

But in modem times the Occident has developed, in addition to this, a very different form of capitalism which has appeared nowhere else: the rational capitalistic organization of (formally) free labour. Only suggestions of it are found elsewhere. Even the organization of unfree labour reached a considerable degree of rationality only on plantations and to a very limited extent in the *Ergasteria* of antiquity. In the manors, manorial workshops, and domestic industries on estates with serf labour it was probably somewhat less developed. Even real domestic industries with free labour have definitely been proved to have existed in only a few isolated cases outside the Occident. The frequent use of day labourers led in a very few cases — especially State monopolies, which are, however, very different from modern industrial organization — to manufacturing organizations, but never to a rational organization of apprenticeship in the handicrafts like that of our Middle Ages.

Rational industrial organization, attuned to a regular market, and neither to political nor irrationally speculative opportunities for profit, is not, however, the only peculiarity of Western capitalism. The modern rational organization of the capitalistic enterprise would not have been possible without two other important factors in its development: the separation of business from the house-

hold, which completely dominates modem economic
life, and closely connected with it, rational book-keeping. A spatial separation of places of work from those of
residence exists elsewhere, as in the Oriental bazaar and
in the *ergasteria* of other cultures. The development of
capitalistic associations with their own accounts is also
found in the Far East, the Near East, and in antiquity.
But compared to the modern independence of business
enterprises, those are only small beginnings. The reason
for this was particularly that the indispensable requisites
for this independence, our rational business book-keeping and our legal separation of corporate from personal
property, were entirely lacking, or had only begun to develop. The tendency everywhere else was for acquisitive
enterprises to arise as parts of a royal or manorial *house-
hold* (of the *oikos*), which is, as Rodbertus has perceived,
with all its superficial similarity, a fundamentally different, even opposite, development.

However, all these peculiarities of Western capitalism have derived their significance in the last analysis
only from their association with the capitalistic organization of labour. Even what is generally called commer-
cialization, the development of negotiable securities and
the rationalization of speculation, the exchanges, etc., is
connected with it. For without the rational capitalistic
organization of labour, all this, so far as it was possible at
all, would have nothing like the same significance, above
all for the social structure and all the specific problems
of the modem Occident connected with it. Exact calculation—the basis of everything else—is only possible on a
basis of free labour.

And just as, or rather because, the world has known
no rational organization of labour outside the modern
Occident, it has known no rational socialism. Of course,
there has been civic economy, a civic food-supply policy,
mercantilism and welfare policies of princes, rationing,
regulation of economic life, protectionism, and *lais-
sez-faire* theories (as in China). The world has also known
socialistic and communistic experiments of various
sorts: family, religious, or military communism, State

socialism (in Egypt), monopolistic cartels, and consumers' organizations. But although there have everywhere been civic market privileges, companies, guilds, and all sorts of legal differences between town and country, the concept of the citizen has not existed outside the Occident, and that of the bourgeoisie outside the modern Occident. Similarly, the proletariat as a class could not exist, because there was no rational organization of free labour under regular discipline. Class struggles between creditor and debtor classes; landowners and the landless, serfs, or tenants; trading interests and consumers or landlords, have existed everywhere in various combinations. But even the Western medieval struggles between putters-out and their workers exist elsewhere only in beginnings. The modern conflict of the large-scale industrial entrepreneur and free-wage labourers was entirely lacking. And thus there could be no such problems as those of socialism.

Hence in a universal history of culture the central problem for us is not, in the last analysis, even from a purely economic view-point, the development of capitalistic activity as such, differing in different cultures only in form: the adventurer type, or capitalism in trade, war, politics, or administration as sources of gain. It is rather the origin of this sober bourgeois capitalism with its rational organization of free labour. Or in terms of cultural history, the problem is that of the origin of the Western bourgeois class and of its peculiarities, a problem which is certainly closely connected with that of the origin of the capitalistic organization of labour, but is not quite the same thing. For the bourgeois as a class existed prior to the development of the peculiar modern form of capitalism, though, it is true, only in the Western hemisphere.

Now the peculiar modern Western form of capitalism has been, at first sight, strongly influenced by the development of technical possibilities. Its rationality is today essentially dependent on the calculability of the most important technical factors. But this means fundamentally that it is dependent on the peculiarities of modern science, especially the natural sciences based on mathematics and exact and rational experiment. On the other hand, the development of these sciences and of the technique resting upon them now receives important stimulation from these capitalistic interests in its practical economic application. It is true that the origin of Western science cannot be attributed to such interests. Calculation, even with decimals, and algebra have been carried on in India, where the decimal system was invented. But it was only made use of by developing capitalism in the West, while in India it led to no modern arithmetic or book-keeping. Neither was the origin of mathematics and mechanics determined by capitalistic interests. But the *technical* utilization of scientific knowledge, so important for the living conditions of the mass of people, was certainly encouraged by economic considerations, which were extremely favourable to it in the Occident. But this encouragement was derived from the peculiarities of the social structure of the Occident. We must hence ask, from *what* parts of that structure was it derived, since not all of them have been of equal importance?

Among those of undoubted importance are the rational structures of law and of administration. For modern rational capitalism has need, not only of the technical means of production, but of a calculable legal system and of administration in terms of formal rules. Without it adventurous and speculative trading capitalism and all sorts of politically determined capitalisms are possible, but no rational enterprise under individual initiative, with fixed capital and certainty of calculations. Such a legal system and such administration have been available for economic activity in a comparative state of legal and formalistic perfection only in the Occident. We must hence inquire where that law came from. Among other circumstances, capitalistic interests have in turn undoubtedly also helped, but by no means alone nor even principally, to prepare the way for the predominance in law and administration of a class of jurists specially trained in rational law. But these interests did not themselves create that law. Quite different forces were at work in this development. And why did not the capitalistic interests do the same in China or India? Why did not the scientific, the artistic, the political, or the economic development there enter upon that path of rationalization which is peculiar to the Occident?

For in all the above cases it is a question of the specific and peculiar rationalism of Western culture. Now by this term very different things may be understood, as the following discussion will repeatedly show. There is, for example, rationalization of mystical contemplation, that is of an attitude which, viewed from other departments of life, is specifically irrational, just as much as there are rationalizations of economic life, of technique, of scientific research, of military training, of law and administration. Furthermore, each one of these fields may be rationalized in terms of very different ultimate values and ends, and what is rational from one point of view may well be irrational from another. Hence rationalizations of the most varied character have existed in various departments of life and in all areas of culture. To characterize their differences from the view-point of cultural history it is necessary to know what departments are rationalized, and in what direction. It is hence our first concern to work out and to explain genetically the special peculiarity of Occidental rationalism, and within this field that of the modern Occidental form. Every such attempt at explanation must, recognizing the fundamental importance of the economic factor, above all take account of the economic conditions. But at the same time the opposite correlation must not be left out of consideration. For though the development of economic rationalism is partly dependent on rational technique and law, it is at the same time determined by the ability and disposition of men to adopt certain types of practical rational conduct. When these types have been obstructed by spiritual obstacles, the development of rational economic conduct has also met serious inner resistance. The magical and religious forces, and the ethical ideas of duty based upon them, have in the past always been among the most important formative influences on conduct. In the studies collected here we shall be concerned with these forces.

Two older essays have been placed at the beginning which attempt, at one important point, to approach the side of the problem which is generally most difficult to grasp: the influence of certain religious ideas on the development of an economic spirit, or the *ethos* of an economic system. In this case we are dealing with the connection of the spirit of modern economic life with the rational ethics of ascetic Protestantism. Thus we treat here only one side of the causal chain. The later studies on the Economic Ethics of the World Religions attempt, in the form of a survey of the relations of the most important religions to economic life and to the social stratification of their environment, to follow out both causal relationships, so far as it is necessary in order to find points of comparison with the Occidental development. For only in this way is it possible to attempt a causal evaluation of those elements of the economic ethics of the Western religions which differentiate them from others, with a hope of attaining even a tolerable degree of approximation. Hence these studies do not claim to be complete analyses of cultures, however brief. On the contrary, in every culture they quite deliberately emphasize the elements in which it differs from Western civilization. They are, hence, definitely oriented to the problems which seem important for the understanding of Western culture from *this* view-point. With our object in view, any other procedure did not seem possible. But to avoid misunderstanding we must here lay special emphasis on the limitation of our purpose. In another respect the uninitiated at least must be warned against exaggerating the importance of these investigations. The Sinologist, the Indologist, the Semitist, or the Egyptologist, will of course find no facts unknown to him. We only hope that he will find nothing definitely wrong in points that are essential. How far it has been possible to come as near this ideal as a non-specialist is able to do, the author cannot know. It is quite evident that anyone who is forced to rely on translations, and furthermore on the use and evaluation of monumental, documentary, or literary sources, has to rely himself on a specialist literature which is often highly controversial, and the merits of which he is unable to judge accurately. Such a writer must make modest claims for the value of his work. All the more so since the number of available translations of real sources (that is, inscriptions and documents) is, especially for China, still very small in comparison with what exists and is important. From all this follows the definitely provisional character of these studies, and especially of the parts dealing with Asia. Only the specialist is entitled to a final judgment. And, naturally, it is only because expert studies with this special purpose and from this particular view-point have not hitherto been made, that the present ones have been written at all. They are destined to be superseded in a much more important sense than this can be said, as it can be, of all scientific work. But however objectionable it may be, such trespassing on other special fields cannot be avoided in comparative work. But one must take the consequences by resigning oneself to considerable doubts regarding the degree of one's success. Fashion and the zeal of the literati would have us think that the specialist can today be spared, or degraded to a position subordinate to that of the seer. Almost all sciences owe something to dilettantes, often very valuable view-points. But dilettantism as a leading principle would be the end of science. He who yearns for seeing should go to the cinema, though it will be offered to him copiously today in literary form in the present field of investigation also. Nothing is farther from the intent of these thoroughly serious studies than such an attitude. And, I might add, whoever wants a sermon should go to a conventicle. The question of the relative value of the cultures which are compared here will not receive a single word. It is true that the path of human destiny cannot but appall him who surveys a section of it. But he will do well to keep his small personal commentaries to himself, as one does at the sight of the sea or of majestic mountains, unless he knows himself to be called and gifted to give them expression in artistic or prophetic form. In most other cases the voluminous talk about intuition does nothing but conceal a lack of perspective toward the object, which merits the same judgment as a similar lack of perspective toward men.

Some justification is needed for the fact that ethnographical material has not been utilized to anything like the extent which the value of its contributions naturally demands in any really thorough investigation, especially of Asiatic religions. This limitation has not only been imposed because human powers of work are restricted. This omission has also seemed to be permissible because we are here necessarily dealing with the religious ethics of the classes which were the culture-bearers of their respective countries. We are concerned with the influence which *their* conduct has had. Now it is quite true that this can only be completely known in all its details when the facts from ethnography and folk-lore have been compared with it. Hence we must expressly admit and emphasize that this is a gap to which the ethnographer will legitimately object. I hope to contribute something to the closing of this gap in a systematic study of the Sociology of Religion. But such an undertaking would have transcended the limits of this investigation with its closely circumscribed purpose. It has been necessary to be content with bringing out the points of comparison with our Occidental religions as well as possible.

Finally, we may make a reference to the *anthropological* side of the problem. When we find again and again that, even in departments of life apparently mutually independent, certain types of rationalization have developed in the Occident, and only there, it would be natural to suspect that the most important reason lay in differences of heredity. The author admits that he is inclined to think the importance of biological heredity very great. But in spite of the notable achievements of anthropological research, I see up to the present no way of exactly or even approximately measuring either the extent or, above all, the form of its influence on the development investigated here. It must be one of the tasks of sociological and historical investigation first to analyse all the influences and causal relationships which can satisfactorily be explained in terms of reactions to environmental conditions. Only then, and when comparative racial neurology and psychology shall have progressed beyond their present and in many ways very promising beginnings, can we hope for even the probability of a satisfactory answer to that problem. In the meantime that condition seems to me not to exist, and an appeal to heredity would therefore involve a premature renunciation of the possibility of knowledge attainable now, and would shift the problem to factors (at present) still unknown.

PART I:
THE PROBLEM

Chapter I.

RELIGIOUS AFFILIATION AND SOCIAL STRATIFICATION

A glance at the occupational statistics of any country of mixed religious composition brings to light with remarkable frequency a situation which has several times provoked discussion in the Catholic press and literature, and in Catholic congresses in Germany, namely, the fact that business leaders and owners of capital, as well as the higher grades of skilled labor, and even more the higher technically and commercially trained personnel of modern enterprises, are overwhelmingly Protestant. This is true not only in cases where the difference in religion coincides with one of nationality, and thus of cultural development, as in Eastern Germany between Germans and Poles. The same thing is shown in the figures of religious affiliation almost wherever capitalism, at t he time of its great expansion, has had a free hand to alter the social distribution of the population in accordance with its needs, and to determine its occupational structure. The more freedom it has had, the more clearly is the effect shown. It is true that the greater relative participation of Protestants in the ownership of capital, in management, and the upper ranks of labor in great modern industrial and commercial enterprises, may in part be explained in terms of historical circumstances, which extend far back into the past, and in which religious affiliation is not a cause of the economic conditions, but to a certain extent appears to be a result of them. Participation in the above economic functions usually involves some previous ownership of ca pital, and generally an expensive education; often both. These are today largely dependent on the possession of inherited wealth, or at least on a certain degree of material well being. A number of those sections of the old Empire which were most highly developed economically and most favored by natural resources and situation, in particular a majority of the wealthy towns went over to Protestantism in the sixteenth century The results of that circumstance favor the Protestants even today in their struggle for economic existence. There arises thus the historical question: why were the districts of highest economic development at the same time particularly favorable to a revolution in the Church? The answer is by no means so simple as one might think.

The emancipation from economic traditionalism appears, no doubt, to be a factor which would greatly strengthen the tendency to doubt the sanctity of the religious tradition, as of all traditional authorities. But it is necessary to note, what has often been forgotten, that the Reformation meant not the elimination the Church's control over everyday life, but rather the substitution of a new form of control for the previous, one. It meant the repudiation of a control which was very lax, at that time scarcely perceptible in practice, and hardly more than formal, in favor of a regulation, of the whole of conduct which, penetrating to all departments of private and public life, was infinitely., burdensome and earnestly enforced. The rule of the Catholic Church, "punishing the heretic, but indulgent. to the sinner", as it was in the past even more than today, is now tolerated by peoples of thoroughly modern economic character, and was borne by the richest and economically most advanced peoples on earth at about the turn of the fifteenth century. The rule of Calvinism, on the other hand, as it was enforced in the sixteenth century in Geneva and in Scotland, at the turn of the sixteenth and seventeenth centuries in large parts of the Netherlands, in the seventeenth in New England, and for a time in England itself, would be for us the most absolutely unbearable form of ecclesiastical control of the individual which could possibly exist. That was exactly what large numbers of the old commercial aristocracy of those times, in Geneva as well as in Holland and England, felt about it. And what the reformers complained of in those areas of high economic development was not too much supervision of life on the part of the Church, but too little. Now how does it happen that at that time those countries which were most advanced economically, and within them the rising bourgeois middle classes, not only failed to resist this unexampled tyranny of Puritanism, but even developed a heroism in its defense? For bourgeois classes as such have seldom before and never since displayed heroism. It was "the last of our heroisms", as Carlyle, not without reason, has said.

But further, and especially important: it may be, as has been claimed, that the greater participation of Protestants in the positions of ownership and management in modern economic life may today be understood, in part at least, simply as a result of the greater mat erial wealth they have inherited. But there are certain other phenomena which cannot be explained in the same way. Thus, to mention only a few facts: there is a great difference discoverable in Baden, in Bavaria, in Hungary, in the type of higher education which Catholic parents, as opposed to Protestant, give their children. That the percentage of Catholics among the students and graduates of higher educational institutions in general lags behind their proportion of the total population," may, to be sure, be largely explicable in terms of inherited differences of wealth. But among the Catholic graduates themselves the percentage of those graduating from the institutions preparing, in particular, for technical studies and industrial and commercial occupations, but in general from those preparing for middle-class business life, lags still farther behind the percentage of Protestants. On the other hand, Catholics prefer the sort of training which the humanistic Gymnasium affords. That is a circumstance to which the above explanation does not apply, but which, on the contrary, is one reason why so few Catholics are engaged in capitalistic enterprise.

Even more striking is a fact which partly explains the smaller proportion of Catholics among the skilled laborers of modern industry. It is well known that the factory has taken its skilled labor to a large extent from young men in the handicrafts; but this is much more true of Protestant than of Catholic journeymen. Among journeymen, in other words, the Catholics show a stronger propensity to remain in their crafts, that is they more often become master craftsmen, whereas the Protestants are attracted to a larger extent into the factories in order to fill the upper ranks skilled labor and administrative positions. The explanation of these cases is undoubtedly that the mental and spiritual peculiarities acquired from the environment, here the type of education favored by the religious atmosphere of the home community and the parental home, have determined the choice of occupation, and through it the professional career.

The smaller participation of Catholics in the modern business life of Germany is all the mo re striking because it runs counter to a tendency which has been observed at all times including the present. National or religious minorities which are in a position of subordination to a group of rulers are likely, through their voluntary or involuntary exclusion from positions of political influence, to be driven with peculiar force into economic activity. Their ablest members seek to satisfy the desire for recognition of their abilities in this field, since there is no opportunity in the service of the State. This has undoubtedly been true of the Poles in Russia and Eastern Prussia, who have without question been undergoing a more rapid economic advance than in Galicia, where they have been in the ascendant. It has in earlier times been true of the Huguenots in France under Louis XIV, the Nonconformists and Quakers in England, and, last but not least, the Jew for two thousand years. But the Catholics in Germany have shown no striking evidence of such a result of their position. In the past they have, unlike the Protestants, undergone no particularly prominent economic development in the times when they, were persecuted or only tolerated, either in Holland or in England. On the other hand, it is a fact that the Protestants (especially certain branches of the movement to be fully discussed later) both as ruling classes and as ruled, both as majority and as minority, have shown a special tendency to develop economic rationalism which cannot be observed to the same extent among Catholics either in the one situation or in the other. Thus the principal explanation of this difference must be sought in the permanent intrinsic character of their religious beliefs, and not only in their temporary external historico-political situations. It will be our task to investigate these religions with a view to finding out what peculiarities they have or have had which might have resulted in the behavior we have described. On superficial analysis, and on the basis of certain current impressions, one might be tempted to express the difference by saying that the greater other-worldliness of Catholicism, the ascetic character of its highest ideals, must have brought up its adherents to a greater indifference toward the good things of this world. Such an explanation f its the popular tendency in the judgment of both religions. On the Protestant side it is used as a basis of criticism of those (real or imagined) ascetic ideals of the 'Catholic way of life, while the Catholics answer with the accusation that materialism results from the secularization of all ideals through Protestantism. One recent writer has attempted to formulate the difference of their attitudes toward economic life in the following manner: "The Catholic is quieter, having less of the acquisitive impulse; he prefers a life of the greatest possible security, even with a smaller income, to a life of risk and excitement, even though it may bring the chance of gaining honor and riches. The proverb says jokingly, 'either eat well or sleep well'. In the present case the Protestant prefers to eat well, the Catholic to sleep undisturbed."

In fact, this desire to eat well may be a correct though incomplete characterization of the motives of many nominal Protestants in Germany at the present time. But things were very different in the past: the English, Dutch, and American Puritans were characterized by the exact opposite of the joy of living, a fact which is indeed, as we shall see, most important for our present study. Moreover, the French Protestants, among others, long retained, and retain to a certain extent up to the present, the characteristics which were impressed upon the Calvinistic Churches everywhere, especially under the cross in the time of the religious struggles. Nevertheless (or was it, perhaps, as we shall ask later, precisely on that account?) it is well known that these characteristics were one of the most important factors in the industrial and capitalistic development of France, and on th e small scale permitted them by their persecution remained so. If we may call this seriousness and the strong predominance of religious interests in the whole conduct of life otherworldliness, then the French Calvinists were and still are at least as otherworldly as, for instance, the North German Catholics, to whom their Catholicism is undoubtedly as vital a matter as religion is to any other people in the world. Both differ from the predominant religious trends in their respective countries in much the same way. The Catholics of France are, in their lower ranks, greatly interested in the enjoyment of life, in the upper directly hostile to religion. Similarly, the Protestants of Germany are today absorbed in worldly economic life, and their upper ranks are most indifferent to religion. Hardly anything shows so clearly as this parallel that, with such vague ideas as that of the alleged otherworldliness of Catholicism, and the alleged materialistic joy of living of Protestantism, and others like them, nothing can be accomplished for our purpose. In such general terms the distinction does not even adequately fit the facts of today, and certainly not of the past. If, however, one wishes to make use of it at all, several other observations present themselves at once which, combined with the above remarks, suggest that the supposed conflict between other-worldliness, asceticism, and ecclesiastical piety on the one side, and participation in capitalistic acquisition on the other, might actually turn out to be an intimate relationship. As a matter of fact it is surely remarkable, to begin with quite a superficial observation, how large is the number of representatives of the most spiritual forms of Christian piety who have sprung from commercial circles. In particular, very many of the most zealous adherents of Pietism are of this origin. It might e explained as a sort of reaction against mammonism on the part of sensitive natures not adapted to commercial life, and, as in the case of Francis of Assisi, man Pietists have themselves interpreted the process of their conversion in these terms. Similarly, the remarkable circumstance that so many of the greatest capitalistic entrepreneurs-down to Cecil Rhodes-have come from clergymen's families might be explained reaction against their ascetic upbringing. But this form of explanation fails where an extraordinary capitalistic business sense is combined in the same persons and groups with the most intensive forms of a piety which penetrates and dominates their whole lives. Such cases are not isolated, but these traits are characteristic of many of the most important Churches and sects in the history of Protestantism. Especially Calvinism, wherever it has appeared, has shown this combination. However little, in the ti me of the expansion of the Reformation, it (or any other Protestant belief) was bound up with any particular social class, it is characteristic and in a certain sense typical that in French Huguenot Churches monks and businessmen (merchants, craftsmen) we re particularly numerous among the proselytes, especially at the time of the persecution. Even the Spaniards knew that heresy (i.e. the Calvinism of the Dutch) promoted trade, and this coincides with the opinions which Sir William Petty expressed in his discussion of the reasons for the capitalistic development of the Netherlands. Gothein rightly calls the Calvinistic diaspora the seedbed of capitalistic economy. Even in this case one might consider the decisive factor to be the superiority of the French and Dutch economic cultures from which these communities sprang, or perhaps the immense influence of exile in the breakdown of traditional relationships. But in France the situation was, as we know from Colbert's struggles, the same even in t he seventeenth century. Even Austria, not to speak of other countries, directly imported Protestant craftsmen.

But not all the Protestant denominations seem to have had an equally strong influence in thi s direction. That of Calvinism, even in Germany, was among the strongest, it seems, and the reformed faith more than the others seems to have promoted the development of the spirit of capitalism, in the Wupperthal as well as else-where. Much more so than Lutheranism, as comparison both in general and in particular instances, especially in the Wupperthal, seems to prove. For Scotland, Buckle, and among English poets, Keats have emphasized these same relationships. Even more striking, as it is only nec-essary to mention, is the connection of a religious way of life with the most intensive development of business acumen among those sects whose otherworldliness is proverbial as their wealth, especially the Quakers and the Mennonites. The part which the former have played in England and North America fell to the latter in Ger-many and the Netherlands. That in East Prussia Freder-ick William I tolerated the Mennonites as indispensable to industry, in spite of their absolute refusal to refusal perform military service, is only one of the numerous well-known cases which illustrates the fact, though, con-sidering the character of that monarch, it is one it is one of the most striking. Finally, that this combination of in-tense piety with just as strong a development of business acumen, was also characteristic of the Pietists, common knowledge.

It is only necessary to think of the Rhine country and of Calw. In this purely introductory discussion it is unnecessary to pile up more examples. For these few already all show one thing: that the spirit of hard work, of progress, or whatever else it might may be called, the awakening of which one is inclined to ascribe to Protes-tantism, must not be understood, as there is a tenden-cy to do, as joy of living nor in any other sense as con-nected with the Enlightenment. The old Protestantism of Luther, Calvin, Knox, Voet, had precious little to do with what today is called progress. To whole aspects of modern life which the most extreme religionist would not wish to suppress today, it was directly hostile. If any inner relationship between certain expressions of the old Protestant spirit and modern capitalistic culture is to be found, we must attempt to find it, for better o r worse, not in its alleged more or less materialistic or at least anti-ascetic joy of living, but in its purely religious characteristics. Montesquieu says (*Esprit des Lois*, Book XX, chap. 7) of the English that they "had progressed the farthest of all peoples of the world in three import-ant things: in piety, in commerce, and in freedom". Is it not possible that their commercial superiority and their adaptation to free political institutions are connected in someway with that record of piety which Montesquieu ascribes to them?

A large number of possible relationships, vaguely perceived, occur to us when we put the question in this way. It will now be our task to formulate what occurs to us confusedly as clearly as is possible, considering the inexhaustible diversity to be found in all historical mate-rial. But in order to do this it is necessary to leave behind the vague and general concepts with which we have dealt up to this point, and attempt to Penetrate into the peculiar characteristics of and the differences between those great worlds of religious thought which have ex-isted historically in the various branches of Christianity.

Before we can proceed to that, however, a few re-marks are necessary, first on the peculiarities of the phenomenon of which we are seeking an historical ex-planation, then concerning the sense in which such an explanation is possible at all within the limits of these investigations.

Chapter II.

THE SPIRIT OF CAPITALISM

In the title of this study is used the somewhat pretentious phrase, the *spirit* of capitalism. What is to be understood by it? The attempt to give anything like a definition of it brings out certain difficulties which are in the very nature of this type of investigation.

If any object can be found to which this term can be applied with any understandable meaning, it can only be an historical individual, i.e. a complex of elements associated in historical reality which we unite into a conceptual whole from the standpoint of their cultural significance.

Such an historical concept, however, since it refers in its content to a phenomenon significant for its unique individuality, cannot be defined according to the formula *genus proximum, differentia specifica*, but it must be gradually put together out of the individual parts which are taken from historical reality to make it up. Thus the final and definitive concept cannot stand at the beginning of the investigation, but must come at the end. We must, in other words, work out in the course of the discussion, as its most important result, the best conceptual formulation of what we here understand by the spirit of capitalism, that is the best from the point of view which interests us here. This point of view (the one of which we shall speak later) is, further, by no means the only possible one from which the historical phenomena we are investigating can be analyzed. Other standpoints would, for this as for every historical phenomenon, yield other characteristics as the essential ones. The result is that it is by no means necessary to understand by the spirit of capitalism only what it will come to mean to *us* for the purposes of our analysis. This is a necessary result of the nature of historical concepts which attempt for their methodological purposes not to grasp historical reality in abstract general formulae, but in concrete genetic sets of relations which are inevitably of a specifically unique and individual character.

Thus, if we try to determine the object, the analysis and historical explanation of which we are attempting, it cannot be in the form of a conceptual definition, but at least in the beginning only a provisional description of what is here meant by the spirit of capitalism. Such a description is, however, indispensable in order clearly to understand the object of the investigation. For this purpose we turn to a document of that spirit which contains what we are looking for in almost classical purity, and at the game time has the advantage of being free from all direct relationship to religion, being thus for our purposes, free of preconceptions.

"Remember, that *time* is money. He that can earn ten shillings a day by his labor, and goes abroad, or sits idle, one half of that day, though he spends but, sixpence during his diversion or idleness, ought not reckon *that* the only expense; he has really spent, rather thrown away, five shilling besides.

"Remember, that *credit* is money. If a man lets his money lie in my hands after it is due, he gives me interest, or so much as I can make of it during that time. This amounts to a considerable sum where a man has good and large credit, and makes good use of it.

"Remember, that money is of the prolific, generating nature. Money can beget money, and its offspring can beget more, and so on. Five shillings turned is six, turned again it is seven and three pence, and so on, till it becomes a hundred pounds. The more there is of it, the more it produces every turning, so that the profits rise quicker and quicker. He that kills a breeding sow, destroys all her offspring to the thousandth generation.

He that murders a crown, destroys all that it might have produced, even scores of pounds."

"Remember this saying, *The good paymaster is lord of another man's purse*. He that is known to pay punctually and exactly to the time he, promises, may at any time, and on any occasion, raise all the money his friends can spare. This is sometimes of great use. After industry and frugality, nothing contributes more to the raising of a young man in the world than punctuality and justice in all his dealings; therefore never keep borrowed money an hour beyond the time you promised, lest a disappointment shut up your friend's purse for ever.

"The most trifling actions that affect a man's credit are to be regarded. The sound of your hammer at five in the morning, or eight at night, heard by a creditor, makes him easy six months longer; but if he sees you at a billiard table, or hears your voice at a tavern, when You should be at work, he sends for his money the next day; demands it, before he can receive it, in a lump. 'It shows, besides, that you are mindful of what you owe; it makes you appear a careful as well as an honest man, and that still increases your credit.

"Beware of thinking all your own that you possess, and of living accordingly. It is a mistake that many people who have credit fall into. To prevent this, keep an exact account for some time both of your expenses and your income. If you take the pains at first to mention particulars, it will have this good effect: you will discover how wonderfully small, trifling expenses mount up to large sums, and will discern what might have been, and may for the future be saved, without occasioning any great inconvenience."

"For six pounds a year you may have the use of one hundred pounds, provided you are a man of known prudence and honesty.

"He that spends a groat a day idly, spends idly above six pounds a year, which is the price for the use of one hundred pounds.

"He that wastes idly a groat's worth of his time per day, one day with another, wastes the privilege of using one hundred pounds each day.

"He that idly loses five shillings' worth of time, loses five shillings, and might as prudently throw five shillings into the sea.

"He that loses five shillings, not only loses that sum, but all the advantage that might be made by turning it in dealing, which by the time that a young man become: old, will amount to a considerable sum of money."

It is Benjamin Franklin who preaches to us in these sentences, the same which Ferdinand Kurnberger satirizes in his clever and malicious *Picture of American Culture* as the supposed confession of faith of the Yankee. That it is the spirit of capitalism which here speaks in characteristic fashion, no one will doubt, however little we may wish to claim that everything which could be understood as pertaining to that spirit is Contained in it. Let us pause a moment to consider this passage, the philosophy of which Kurnberger sums up in the words, "They make tallow out of cattle and money out of men". The peculiarity of this philosophy of avarice appears to be the ideal of the honest man of recognized credit, and above all the idea of a duty of the individual toward the increase of his capital, which is assumed as an end in itself. Truly what is here preached is not simply a means of making one's way in the world, but a peculiar ethic. The infraction of its rules is treated not as foolishness but as forgetfulness of duty. That is the essence of the matter. It is not mere business astuteness, that sort of thing is common enough, it is an ethos. *This* is the quality which interests us.

When Jacob Fugger, in speaking to a business associate who had retired and who wanted to persuade him to do the same, since he had made enough money and should let others have a chance, rejected that as Pusillanimity and answered that "he (Fugger) thought otherwise, he wanted to make money as long as he could", the spirit of his statement is evidently quite different from that of Franklin. What in the former case was an expression of commercial daring and a Personal inclination morally neutral, in the latter takes on the character of ethically colored maxim for the conduct of life. The concept spirit of capitalism is here used in this specific sense, it is the spirit of modern capitalism. For that we are here dealing only with Western European and American capitalism is obvious from the way in which the problem was stated. Capitalism existed in China, India, Babylon, in the classic world, and in the Middle Ages. But in all these cases, as we shall see, this particular ethos was lacking.

Now, all Franklin's moral attitudes are colored with utilitarianism. Honesty is useful, because it assures credit; so are punctuality, industry, frugality, and that is the reason they are virtues. A logical deduction from this would be that where, for instance, the appearance of honesty serves the same purpose, that would suffice, and an unnecessary surplus of this virtue would evidently appear to Franklin's eyes a unproductive waste. And as a matter of fact, the story in his autobiography of his conversion to those virtues, or the discussion of the value of a strict maintenance of the appearance of modesty, the assiduous belittlement of one's own deserts in order to gal general recognition later, confirms this impression. According to Franklin, those virtues, like all others, are only in so far virtues as they are actually useful to t individual, and the surrogate of mere appearance always sufficient when it accomplishes the end view. It is a conclusion which is inevitable for strict utilitarianism. The impression of many Germans t the virtues professed by Americanism are pure hypocrisy seems to have been confirmed by this striking case. But in fact the matter is not by any means so simple.

Benjamin Franklin's own character, as it appears in the really unusual candidness of his autobiography, belies that suspicion. The circumstance that he ascribes his recognition of the utility of virtue to a divine revelation which was intended to lead him in the path of righteousness, shows that something more than mere garnishing for purely egocentric motives is involved.

In fact, the *summum bonum* of his ethic, the earning of more and more money, combined with the strict avoidance of all spontaneous enjoyment of life, is above all completely devoid of any eudaemonistic, not to say hedonistic, admixture. It is thought of so purely as an end in itself, that from the point of view of the happiness of, or utility to, the single individual, it appears entirely transcendental and absolutely irrational. Man is dominated by the making of money, by acquisition as the ultimate purpose of his life. Economic acquisition is no longer subordinated to man as the means for the satisfaction of his material needs. This reversal of what we should call the natural relationship, so irrational from a naive point of view, is evidently as definitely a leading principle of capitalism as it is foreign to all peoples not under capitalistic influence. At the same time it expresses a type of feeling which is closely connected with certain religious ideas. If we thus ask, *why* should "money be made out of men", Benjamin Franklin himself, although he was a colorless deist, answers in his autobiography with a quotation from the Bible, which his strict Calvinistic father drummed into him again and again in his youth: "Seest thou a man diligent in his business? He shall stand before kings" (Prov. xxii. 29). The earning of money within the modern economic order is, so long as it is done legally, the result and the expression of virtue and proficiency in a calling; and this virtue and proficiency are, as it is now not difficult to see, the real Alpha and Omega of Franklin's ethic, as expressed in the passages we have quoted, as well as in all his works without exception.

And in truth this peculiar idea, so familiar to us today, but in reality so little a matter of course, of one's duty in a calling, is what is most characteristic of the social ethic of capitalistic culture, and is in a sense the fundamental basis of it. It is an obligation which the individual is supposed to feel and does feel towards the content of his professional activity, no matter in what it consists, in particular no matter whether it appears on the surface as a utilization of his personal powers, or only of his material possessions (as capital).

Of course, this conception has not appeared only under capitalistic conditions. On the contrary, we shall, later trace its origins back to a time previous to the advent of capitalism. Still less, naturally, do we maintain:' that a conscious acceptance of these ethical maxims on the part of the individuals, entrepreneurs or laborers in modem capitalistic enterprises, is a condition o the further existence of present day capitalism. The capitalistic economy of the present day is an immense cosmos into which the individual is born, and which presents itself to him, at least as an individual, as an unalterable order of things in which he must live. It forces the individual, in so far as he is involved in the system of market relationships, to conform to capitalistic rules of action. The manufacturer who in the long run acts counter to these norms, will just as inevitably be eliminated from the economic scene as the worker who cannot or will not adapt himself to them will be thrown into the streets without a job.

Thus the capitalism of today, which has come t dominate economic life, educates and selects the economic subjects which it needs through a process of economic survival of the fittest. But here one can easily see the limits of the concept of selection as a means of historical explanation. In order that a manner of life so well adapted to the peculiarities of capitalism could be selected at all, i.e. should come to dominate others, it had to originate somewhere, and not in isolated individuals alone, but as a way of life common to whole groups of men. This origin is what really needs explanation. Concerning the doctrine of the more naive historical materialism, that such ideas originate as a reflection or superstructure of economic situations, we shall speak more in detail below. At this point it will suffice for our purpose to call attention to the fact that without doubt, in the country of Benjamin Franklin's birth (Massachusetts), the spirit of capitalism (in the sense we have attached to it) was present before the capitalistic order. There were complaints of a peculiarly Calculating sort of profit seeking in New England, as distinguished from other parts of America, as early as 1632. It is further undoubted that capitalism remained far less developed in some of the neighboring colonies, the later Southern States of the United States of America, in spite of the fact that these latter were founded by large capitalists for business motives, while the New England colonies were founded by preachers and seminary graduates with the help of small bourgeois, craftsmen and yoemen, for religious reasons. In this case the causal relation is certainly the reverse of that suggested by the materialistic standpoint.

But the origin and history of such ideas is much more complex than the theorists of the superstructure suppose. The spirit of capitalism, in the sense in which we are using the term, had to fight its way to supremacy against a whole world of hostile forces. A state of mind such as that expressed in the passages we have quoted from Franklin, and which called forth the applause of a whole people, would both in ancient times and in the Middle Ages have been proscribed as the lowest sort of avarice and as an attitude entirely lacking in self respect. It is, in ' fact, still regularly thus looked upon by all those social groups which are least involved in or adapted to modern capitalistic conditions. This is not wholly because the instinct of acquisition was in those times unknown or undeveloped, as has often been said. Nor because the *auri sacra fames*, the greed for gold, was then, or now, less powerful outside of bourgeois capitalism than within its peculiar sphere, as the illusions of modern romanticists are wont to believe. The difference between the capitalistic and pre-capitalistic spirits is not to be found at this point. The greed of the Chinese Mandarin, the old Roman aristocrat, or the modern peasant, can stand up to any comparison. And the *auri sacra fames* of a Neapolitan cab driver or *barcaiuolo*, and certainly of Asiatic representatives of similar trades, as well as of the craftsmen of southern European or Asiatic countries is, as anyone can find out for himself, very much more intense, and especially more unscrupulous than that of, say, an Englishman in similar circumstances.

The universal reign of absolute unscrupulousness in the pursuit of selfish interests by the making of money has been a specific characteristic of precisely those countries whose bourgeois-capitalistic development, measured according to Occidental standards, has remained backward. As every employer knows, the lack of *coscienziosita* of the labourers of such countries, for instance Italy as compared with Germany, has been, and to a certain extent still is, one of the principal obstacles to their capitalistic development. Capitalism cannot make use of the labor of those who practice the doctrine of undisciplined *liberum arbitrium*, any more than it can make use of the business man who seems absolutely unscrupulous in his dealings with others, as we can learn from Franklin. Hence the difference does not lie in the degree of development of any impulse to make money. The *auri sacra fames* is as old as the history of man. But we shall see that those who submitted to it without reserve as an uncontrolled impulse, such as the Dutch sea captain who "would go through hell for gain, even though he scorched his sails", were by no means the representatives of that attitude of mind from which the specifically modern capitalistic spirit as a mass phenomenon is derived, and that is what matters. At all periods of history, wherever it was possible, there has been ruthless acquisition, bound to, no ethical norms whatever. Like war and piracy, trade has often been unrestrained in its relations with foreigners and those outside the group. The double ethic has permitted here what was forbidden in dealings among brothers.

Capitalistic acquisition as an adventure has been at home in all types of economic society which have known trade with the use of money and which have offered it opportunities, through *commenda*, farming of taxes, State loans, financing of wars, ducal courts and office holders. Likewise the inner attitude of the adventurer, which laughs at all ethical limitations, has been universal. Absolute and conscious ruthlessness in acquisition has often stood in the closest connection with the strictest conformity to tradition. Moreover, with the breakdown of tradition and the more or less complete extension of free economic enterprise, even to within the social group, the new thing has not generally been ethically justified and encouraged, but only tolerated as a fact. And this fact has been treated either as ethically indifferent or as reprehensible, but unfortunately unavoidable. This has not only been the normal attitude of all ethical teachings, but, what is more important, also that expressed in the practical action of the average man of pre-capitalistic times, pre-capitalistic in the sense that the rational utilization of capital in a permanent enterprise and the rational capitalistic organization of labor had not yet become dominant forces in the determination of economic activity. Now just this attitude was one of the strongest inner obstacles which the adaptation of men to the conditions of an ordered bourgeois-capitalistic economy has encountered everywhere.

The most important opponent with which the spirit of capitalism, in the sense of a definite standard of life claiming ethical sanction, has had to struggle, was that type of attitude and reaction to new situations which we may designate as traditionalism. In this case also every attempt at a final definition must be held in abeyance. On the other hand, lye must try to make the provisional meaning clear by citing a few cases. We will begin from below, with the laborers.

One of the technical means which the modern employer uses in order to secure the greatest possible amount of work from his men is the device of piece rates. In agriculture, for instance, the gathering of the harvest is a case where the greatest possible intensity of labor is called for, since, the weather being uncertain, the difference between high profit and heavy loss may depend on the speed with which the harvesting can be done. Hence a system of piece rates is almost universal in this case. And since the interest of the employer in a speeding. up of harvesting increases with the increase of the results and the intensity of the work, the attempt has again and again been made, by increasing the piece rates of the workmen, thereby giving them an opportunity to earn what is for them a very high wage, to interest them in increasing their own efficiency. But a Peculiar difficulty has been met with surprising frequency: raising the Piece rates has often had the result that not more but less has been accomplished in the same time, because the worker reacted to the increase not by increasing but by decreasing the amount of his work. A man, for instance, who at the rate of 1 mark per acre mowed 2 1/2 acres per day and earned 2 1/2 marks, when the rate was raised to 1.25 marks per acre mowed, not 3 acres, as be might easily have done, thus earning 3.75 marks, but only 2 acres, so that he could still earn the 2 1/2 marks to which he was accustomed. The opportunity of earning more was less attractive than that of working less. He did not ask: how much can I earn in a day if 1 do as much work as possible? but: how much must 1 work in order to cam the wage, 2 1/2 marks, which I earned before and which takes care of my traditional needs? This is an example of what is here meant by traditionalism. A man does not "by nature" wish to cam more and more money, but simply to live as he is accustomed to live and to earn as much as is necessary for that purpose. Wherever modern capitalism has begun its work of increasing the productivity of human labor by increasing its intensity, it has encountered the immensely stubborn resistance of this leading trait of pre-capitalistic labor. And today it encounters it the more, the more backward (from a capitalistic point of view) the laboring forces are with which it has to deal.

Another obvious possibility, to return to our example, since the appeal to the acquisitive instinct through higher wage rates failed, would have been to try the opposite policy, to force the worker by reduction of his wage rates to work harder to cam the same amount than he did before. Low wages and high profits seem even today to a superficial observer to stand in correlation; everything which is paid out in wages seems to involve a corresponding reduction of profits. That road capitalism has taken again and again since its beginning ' For centuries it was an article of faith, that low wages were productive, i.e. that they increased the material results of labor so that, as Pieter de la Cour, on this point, as we shall see, quite in the spirit of the old Calvinism, said long ago, the people only work because and so long as they are poor.

But the effectiveness of this apparently so efficient method has its limits. Of course the presence of a surplus population which it can hire cheaply in the labour market is a necessity for the development of Capitalism. But though too large a reserve army may in certain cases favor its quantitative expansion, it checks its qualitative development, especially the transition to types of enterprise which make more intensive use of labor. Low wages are by no means identical with cheap labor. From a purely quantitative point of view the efficiency of labor decreases with a wage which is physiologically insufficient, which may in the long run even mean a survival of the unfit. The present day average Silesian mows, when he exerts himself to the full, little more than two thirds as much land as the better paid and nourished Pomeranian or Mecklenburger, and the Pole, the further East he comes from, accomplishes progressively less than the German. Low wages fail even from a purely business point of view wherever it is a question of producing goods which require any sort of skilled labor, or the use of expensive machinery which is easily damaged, or in general wherever any great amount of sharp attention or of initiative is required. Here low wages do not pay, and their effect is the opposite of what was intended. For not only is a developed sense of responsibility absolutely indispensable, but in general also an attitude which, at least during working hours, is freed from continual calculations of how the customary wage May be earned with a maximum of comfort and a minimum of exertion. Labor must, on the contrary, be performed as if it were an absolute end in itself, a calling. But such an attitude is by no means a product of nature. It cannot be evoked by low wages or high ones alone, but can only be the product of a long and arduous process of education.

Today, capitalism, once in the saddle, can recruit its laboring force in all industrial countries with comparative ease. In the past this was in every case an extremely difficult problem. And even today it could probably not get along without the support of a powerful ally along the way, which, as we shall see below, was at hand at the time of its development.

What is meant can again best be explained by means of an example. The type of backward traditional form of labor is today very often exemplified by women workers, especially unmarried ones. An almost universal complaint of employers of girls, for instance German girls, is that they are almost entirely unable and unwilling to give up methods of work inherited or once learned in favor of more efficient ones, to adapt themselves to new methods, to learn and to concentrate their intelligence, or even to use it at all. Explanations of the possibility of making work easier, above all more profitable to themselves, generally encounter a complete lack of understanding. Increases of piece rates are without avail against the stone wall of habit. In general it is otherwise, and that is a point of no little importance from our viewpoint, only with girls having a specifically religious, especially a Pietistic, background. One often bears, and statistical investigation confirms it, that by far the best chances of economic education are found among this group. The ability of mental concentration, as well as the absolutely essential feeling of obligation to one's job, are here most often combined with a strict economy which calculates the possibility of high earnings, and a cool self-control and frugality which enormously increase performance. This provides the most favorable foundation for the conception of labor as an end in itself, as a calling which is necessary to capitalism: the chances of overcoming traditionalism are greatest on account of the religious upbringing. This observation of present-day capitalism in itself suggests that it is worth while to ask how this connection of adaptability to capitalism with religious factors may have come about in the days of the early development of capitalism. For that they were even then present in much the same form can be inferred from numerous facts. For instance, the dislike and the persecution which Methodist workmen in the eighteenth century met at the hands of their comrades were not solely nor even principally the result of their religious eccentricities, England had seen many of those and more striking ones. It rested rather, as the destruction of their tools, repeatedly mentioned in the reports, suggests, upon their specific willingness to work as we should say today.

However, let us again return to the present, and this time to the entrepreneur, in order to clarify the meaning of traditionalism in his case. Sombart, in his discussions of the genesis of capitalism, has distinguished between the satisfaction of needs and acquisition as the two great leading principles in economic history. In the former case the attainment of the goods necessary to meet personal needs, in the latter a struggle for profit free from the limits set by needs, have been the ends controlling the form and direction of economic activity. What he called the economy of needs seems at first glance to be identical with what is here described as economic traditionalism. That may be the case if the concept of needs is limited to traditional needs. But if that is not done, a number of economic types which must be considered capitalistic according to the definition of capital which Sombart gives in another part of his work, would be excluded from the category of acquisitive economy and put into that of needs economy. Enterprises, namely, which are carried on by private entrepreneurs by utilizing capital (money or goods with a money value) to make a profit, purchasing the means of production and selling the product, i.e. undoubted capitalistic enterprises, may at the same time have a traditionalistic character. This has, in the course even of modem economic history, not been merely an occasional case, but rather the rule, with continual interruptions from repeated and increasingly powerful conquests of the capitalistic spirit. To be sure the capitalistic form of an enterprise and the spirit in which it is run generally stand in some sort of adequate relationship to each other, but not In one of necessary interdependence. Nevertheless, we provisionally use the expression spirit of (modern) capitalism to describe that attitude which seeks profit rationally and systematically in the manner which we have illustrated, by the example of Benjamin Franklin. This, however, is justified by the historical fact that that attitude of mind has on the one hand found its most suitable expression in capitalistic enterprise, while on the other the enterprise has derived its most suitable motive force from the spirit of capitalism.

But the two may very well occur separately. Benjamin Franklin was filled with the spirit of capitalism at a time when his printing business did not differ in form from any handicraft enterprise. And we shall see that at the beginning of modem times it was by no means the capitalistic entrepreneurs of the commercial aristocracy, who were either the sole or the predominant bearers of the attitude we have here called the spirit of capitalism. It was much more the rising strata of the lower industrial middle classes. Even in the nineteenth century its classical representatives were not the elegant gentlemen of Liverpool and Hamburg, with their commercial fortunes handed down for generations, but the self-made parvenus of Manchester and Westphalia, who often rose from very modest circumstances. As early as the sixteenth century the situation was similar; the industries which arose at that time were mostly created by parvenus .

The management, for instance, of a bank, a wholesale export business, a large retail establishment, or of a large putting-out enterprise dealing with goods produced in homes, is certainly only possible in the form of a capitalistic enterprise. Nevertheless, they may all be carried on in a traditionalistic spirit. In fact, the business of a large bank of issue cannot be carried on in any other way. The foreign trade of whole epochs has rested on the basis of monopolies and legal privileges Of strictly traditional character. In retail trade -- and we are not here talking of the small men without capital who are continually crying out for Government aid -- the revolution which is making an end of the old traditionalism is still in full swing. It is the same development which broke up the old putting-out system, to which modern domestic labor is related only in form. How this revolution takes place and what is its significance may, in spite of the fact these things are so familiar, be again brought out by a concrete example.

Until about the middle of the past century the life of a putter-out was, at least in many of the branches of the Continental textile industry, what we should today consider very comfortable. We may imagine its routine somewhat as follows: The peasants came with their cloth, often (in the case of linen) principally or entirely made from raw material which the peasant himself had produced, to the town in which the putter-out lived, and after a careful, often official, appraisal of the quality, received the customary price for it. The putter-out's customers, for markets any appreciable distance away, were middlemen, who also came to him, generally not yet following samples, but seeking traditional qualities, and bought from his warehouse, or, long before delivery, placed orders which were probably in turn passed on to the peasants. Personal canvassing of customers took place, if at all, only at long intervals. Otherwise correspondence sufficed, though the sending of samples slowly gained ground. The number of business hours was very moderate, perhaps five to six a day, sometimes considerably less; in the rush season, where there was one, more. Earnings were moderate; enough to lead a respectable life and in good times to put away a little. On the whole, relations among competitors were relatively good, with a large degree of agreement on the fundamentals of business. A long daily visit to the tavern, with often plenty to drink, and a congenial circle of friends, made life comfortable and leisurely.

The form of organization was in every respect capitalistic; the entrepreneur's activity was of a purely business character; the use of capital, turned over in the business, was indispensable; and finally, the objective aspect of the economic process, the bookkeeping, was rational. But it was traditionalistic business, if one considers the spirit which animated the entrepreneur: the traditional manner of life, the traditional rate of profit, the traditional amount of work, the traditional manner of regulating the relationships with labor, and the essentially traditional circle of customers and the manner of attracting new ones. All these dominated the conduct of the business, were at the basis, one may say, of the *ethos* of this group of business men.

Now at some time this leisureliness was suddenly destroyed, and often entirely without any essential change in the form of organization, such as the transition to a unified factory, to mechanical weaving, etc. What happened was, on the contrary, often no more than this: some young man from one of the putting-out families went out into the country, carefully chose weavers for his employ, greatly increased the rigor of his supervision of their work, and thus turned them from peasants into laborers. On the other hand, he would begin to change his marketing methods by so far as possible going directly to the final consumer, would take the details into his own hands, would personally solicit customers, visiting them every year, and above all would adapt the quality of the product directly to their needs and wishes. At the same time he began to introduce the principle of low prices and large turnover. There was repeated what everywhere and always is the result of such a process of rationalization: those who would not follow suit had to go out of business. The idyllic state collapsed under the pressure of a bitter competitive struggle, respectable fortunes were made, and not lent out at interest, but always reinvested in the business. The old leisurely and comfortable attitude toward life gave way to a hard frugality in which some participated and came to the top, because they did not wish to consume but to earn, while others who wished to keep on with the old ways were forced to curtail their consumption.

And, what is most important in this connection, it was not generally in such cases a stream of new money invested in the industry which brought about this revolution—in several cases known to me the whole revolutionary process was set in motion with a few thousands of capital borrowed from relations -- but the new spirit, the spirit of modern capitalism, had set to work. The question of the motive forces in the expansion of modern capitalism is not in the first instance a question of the origin of the capital sums which were available for capitalistic uses, but, above all, of the development of the spirit of capitalism. Where it appears and is able to work itself out, it produces its own capital and monetary supplies as the means to its ends, but the reverse is not true. Its entry on the scene was not generally peaceful. A flood of mistrust, sometimes of hatred, above all of moral indignation, regularly opposed itself to the first innovator. Often -- I know of several cases of the sort — regular legends of mysterious shady spots in his previous life have been produced. It is very easy not to recognize that only an unusually strong character could save an entrepreneur of this new type from the loss of his temperate self-control and from both moral and economic shipwreck. Furthermore, along with clarity of vision and ability to it is only by virtue of very definite and highly developed ethical qualities that it has been possible for him to command the absolutely indispensable confidence of his customers and workmen. Nothing else could have given him the strength to overcome the innumerable obstacles, above all the infinitely more intensive work which is demanded of the modern entrepreneur. But these are ethical qualities of quite a different sort from those adapted to the traditionalism of the past.

And, as a rule, it has been neither dare-devil and unscrupulous speculators, economic adventurers such as we meet at all periods of economic history, nor simply great financiers who have carried through this change, outwardly so inconspicuous, but nevertheless so decisive for the penetration of economic life with the new spirit. On the contrary, they were men who had grown up in the hard school of life, calculating and daring at he same time, above all temperate and reliable, shrewd d completely devoted to their business, with strictly bourgeois opinions and principles. One is tempted to think that these personal moral qualities have not the slightest relation to any ethical maxims, to say nothing of religious ideas, but that the essential relation between them is negative. The ability to free oneself from the common tradition, a sort of liberal enlightenment, seems likely to be the most suitable basis for such a business man's success. And today that is generally precisely the case. Any relationship between religious beliefs and conduct is generally absent, and where any exists, at least in Germany, it tends to be of the negative sort. The people filled with the spirit of capitalism today tend to be indifferent, if not hostile, to the Church. The thought of the pious boredom of paradise has little attraction for their active natures; religion appears to them as a means of drawing people away from labor in this world. If you ask them what is the meaning of their restless activity, why they are never satisfied with what they have, thus appearing so senseless to any purely worldly view of life, they would perhaps give the answer, if they know any at all: "to provide for my children and grandchildren". But more often and, since that motive is not peculiar to them, but was just as effective for the traditionalist, more correctly, simply: that business with its continuous work has become a necessary part of their lives. That is in fact the only possible motivation, but it at the same time expresses what is, seen from the viewpoint of personal happiness, so irrational about this sort of life, where a man exists for the sake of his business, instead of the reverse.

Of course, the desire for the power and recognition which the mere fact of wealth brings plays its part. When the imagination of a whole people has once been turned toward purely quantitative bigness, as in the United States, this romanticism of numbers exercises an irresistible appeal to the poets among business men. Otherwise it is in general not the real leaders, and especially not the permanently successful entrepreneurs, who are taken in by it. In particular, the resort to entailed estates and the nobility, with sons whose conduct at the university and in the officers' corps tries to cover up their social origin, as has been the typical history of German capitalistic parvenu families, is a product of later decadence. The ideal type of the capitalistic entrepreneur, as it has been represented even in Germany by occasional outstanding examples, has no relation to such more or less refined climbers. He avoids ostentation and unnecessary expenditure, as well as conscious enjoyment of his power, and is embarrassed by the outward signs of the social recognition which he receives. His manner of life is, in other words, often, and we shall have to investigate the historical significance of just this important fact, distinguished by a certain ascetic tendency, as appears clearly enough in the sermon of Franklin which we have quoted. It is, namely, by no means exceptional, but rather the rule, for him to have a sort of modesty which is essentially more honest than the reserve which Franklin so shrewdly recommends. He gets nothing out of his wealth for himself, except the irrational sense of having done his job well.

But it is just that which seems to the pre-capitalistic man so incomprehensible and mysterious, so unworthy and contemptible. That anyone should be able to make it the sole purpose of his life-work, to sink into the grave weighed down with a great material load of money and goods, seems to him explicable only as the product of a perverse instinct, the *auri sacra fames*.

At present under our individualistic political, legal, and economic institutions, with the forms of organization and general structure which are peculiar to our economic order, this spirit of capitalism might be understandable, as has been said, purely as a result of adaptation. The capitalistic system so needs this devotion to the calling of making money, it is an attitude toward material goods which is so well suited to that system, so intimately bound up with the conditions of survival in the economic struggle for existence, that there can today no longer be any question of a necessary connection of that acquisitive manner of life with any single *Weltanschauung*. In fact, it no longer needs the support of any religious forces, and feels the attempts of religion to influence economic life, in so far as they can still be

felt at all, to be as much an unjustified interference as
its regulation by the State. In such circumstances men's
commercial and social interests do tend to determine
their opinions and attitudes. Whoever does not adapt
his manner of life to the conditions of capitalistic success must go under, or at least cannot rise. But these are
phenomena of a time in which modern capitalism has
become dominant and has become emancipated from
its old supports. But as it could at one time destroy the
old forms of medieval regulation of economic life only
in alliance with the growing power of the modern State,
the same, we may say provisionally, may have been the
case in its relations with religious forces. Whether and in
what sense that was the case, it is our task to investigate.
For that the conception of money-making as an end in
itself to which people were bound, as a calling, was contrary to the ethical feelings of whole epochs, it is hardly necessary to prove. The dogma *Deo placere vix potest*
which was incorporated into the canon law and applied
to the activities of the merchant, and which at that time
(like the passage in the gospel about interest) was considered genuine, as well as St. Thomas's characterization
of the desire for gain as *turpitudo* (which term even included unavoidable and hence ethically justified profit
making), already contained a high degree of concession
on the part of the Catholic doctrine to the financial powers with which the Church had such intimate political
relations in the Italian cities, as compared with the much
more radically anti-chrematistic views of comparatively
wide circles. But even where the doctrine was still better
accommodated to the facts, as for instance with Anthony
of Florence, the feeling was never quite overcome, that
activity directed to acquisition for its own sake was at
bottom a *pudendum* which was to be tolerated only because of the unalterable necessities of life in this world.

Some moralists of that time, especially of the nomi-
nalistic school, accepted developed capitalistic business
forms as inevitable, and attempted to justify them, especially commerce, as necessary. The *industria* developed
in it they were able to regard, though not without con-

tradictions, as a legitimate source of profit, and hence
ethically unobjectionable. But the dominant doctrine
rejected the spirit of capitalistic acquisition as *turpitudo*,
or at least could not give it a positive ethical sanction.
An ethical attitude like that of Benjamin Franklin would
have been simply unthinkable. This was, above all, the
attitude of capitalistic circles themselves. Their life-work
was, so long as they clung to the tradition of the Church,
at best something morally indifferent. It was tolerated,
but was still, even if only on account of the continual
danger of collision with the Church's doctrine on usury,
somewhat dangerous to salvation. Quite considerable
sums, as the sources show, went at the death of rich people to religious institutions as conscience money, at times
even back to former debtors as *usura* which had been
unjustly taken from them. It was otherwise, along with
heretical and other tendencies looked upon with disap-
proval, only in those parts of the commercial aristocracy
which were already emancipated from the tradition. But
even skeptics and people indifferent to the Church often
reconciled themselves with it by gifts, because it was a
sort of insurance against the uncertainties of what might
come after death, or because (at least according to the
very widely held latter view) an external obedience to
the commands of the Church was sufficient to insure salvation. Here the either non moral or immoral character
of their action in the opinion of the participants themselves comes clearly to light.

Now, how could activity, which was at best ethically tolerated, turn into a calling in the sense of Benjamin
Franklin? The fact to be explained historically is that in
the most highly capitalistic center of that time, in Florence of the fourteenth and fifteenth centuries, the money
and capital market of all the great political Powers, this
attitude was considered ethically unjustifiable, or at best
to be tolerated. But in the backwoods small bourgeois
circumstances of Pennsylvania in the eighteenth century, where business threatened for simple lack of money
to fall back into barter, where there was hardly a sign of
large enterprise, where only the earliest beginnings of

banking were to be found, the same thing was considered the essence of moral conduct, even commanded in the name of duty. To speak here of a reflection of material conditions in the ideal superstructure would be patent nonsense. What was the background of ideas which could account for the sort of activity apparently directed toward profit alone as a calling toward which the individual feels himself to have an ethical obligation? For it was this idea which gave the way of life of the new entrepreneur its ethical foundation and justification.

The attempt has been made, particularly by Sombart, in what are often judicious and effective observations, to depict economic rationalism as the salient feature of modern economic life as a whole. Undoubtedly with justification, if by that is meant the extension of the productivity of labor which has, through the subordination of the process of production to scientific points of view, relieved it from its dependence upon the natural organic limitations of the human individual. Now this process of rationalization in the field of technique and economic organization undoubtedly determines an important part of the ideals of life of modern bourgeois society. Labor in the service of a rational organization for the provision of humanity with material goods has without doubt always appeared to representatives of the capitalistic spirit as one of the most important purposes of their life-work. It is only necessary, for instance, to read Franklin's account of his efforts in the service of civic improvements in Philadelphia clearly to apprehend this obvious truth. And the joy and pride of having given employment to numerous people, of having had a part in the economic progress of his home town in the sense referring to figures of population and volume of trade which capitalism associated with the word, all these things obviously are part of the specific and undoubtedly idealistic satisfactions in life to modern men of business. Similarly it is one of the fundamental characteristics of an individualistic capitalistic economy that it is rationalized on the basis of rigorous calculation, directed with foresight and caution toward the economic success which is sought in sharp contrast to the hand-to-mouth existence of the peasant, and to the privileged traditionalism of the guild craftsman and of the adventurers' capitalism, oriented to the exploitation of political opportunities and irrational speculation.

It might thus seem that the development of the spirit of capitalism is best understood as part of the development of rationalism as a whole, and could be deduced from the fundamental position of rationalism on the basic problems of life. In the process Protestantism would only have to be considered in so far as it had formed a stage prior to the development of a purely rationalistic philosophy. But any serious attempt to carry this thesis through makes it evident that such a simple way of putting the question will not work, simply because of the fact that the history of rationalism shows a development which by no means follows parallel lines in the various departments of life. The rationalization of private law, for instance, if it is thought of as a logical simplification and rearrangement of the content of the law, was achieved in the highest hitherto known degree in the Roman law of late antiquity. But it remained most backward in some of the countries with the highest degree of economic rationalization, notably in England, where the Renaissance of Roman Law was overcome by the power of the great legal corporations, while it has always retained its supremacy in the Catholic countries of Southern Europe. The worldly rational philosophy of the eighteenth century did not find favor alone or even principally in the countries of highest capitalistic development. The doctrines of Voltaire are even today the common property of broad upper, and what is practically more important, middle class groups in the Romance Catholic countries. Finally, if under practical rationalism is understood the type of attitude which sees and judges the world consciously in terms of the worldly interests of the individual ego, then this view of life was and is the special peculiarity of the peoples of the *liberum arbitrium*, such as the Italians and the French are in very flesh and blood. But we have already convinced ourselves that this is by no means the soil in which that relationship of a man to his calling as a task, which is necessary to capitalism, has preeminently grown. In fact, one may -- this simple proposition, which is often forgotten, should be placed at the beginning of every study which essays to deal with rationalism -- rationalize life from fundamentally different basic points of view and in very different directions, Rationalism is an historical concept which covers a whole world of different things. It will be our task to find out whose intellectual child the particular concrete form of rational thought was, from which the idea of a calling and the devotion to labor in the calling has grown, which is, as we have seen, so irrational from the standpoint of purely eudaemonistic self interest, but which has been and still is one of the most characteristic elements of our capitalistic culture. We are here particularly interested in the origin of precisely the irrational element which lies in this, as in every conception of a calling.

Chapter III.

LUTHER'S CONCEPTION OF THE CALLING. TASK OF THE INVESTIGATION

Now it is unmistakable that even in the German word *Beruf*, and perhaps still more clearly in the English *calling*, a religious conception, that of a task set by God, is at least suggested. The more emphasis is put upon the word in a concrete case, the more evident is the connotation. And if we trace the history of the word through the civilized languages, it appears that neither the predominantly Catholic peoples nor those of classical antiquity have possessed any expression of similar connotation for what we know as a calling (in the sense of a life-task, a definite field in which to work), while one has existed for all predominantly Protestant peoples. It may be further shown that this is not due to any ethnical peculiarity of the languages concerned. It is not, for instance, the product of a Germanic spirit, but in its modern meaning the word comes from the Bible translations, through the spirit of the translator, not that of the original. In Luther's translation of the Bible it appears to have first been used at a point in Jesus Sirach (x i. 20 and 21) precisely in our modern sense. After that it speedily took on its present meaning in the everyday speech of all Protestant peoples, while earlier not even a suggestion of such a meaning could be found in the secular literature of any of them, and even, in religious writings, so far as I can ascertain, it is only found in one of the German mystics whose influence on Luther is well known.

51

Like the meaning of the word, the idea is new, a product of the Reformation. This may be assumed as generally known. It is true that certain suggestions of the positive valuation of routine activity in the world, which is contained in this conception of the calling, had already existed in the Middle Ages, and even in late Hellenistic antiquity. We shall speak of that later. But at least one thing was unquestionably new: the valuation of the fulfillment of duty in worldly affairs as the highest form which the moral activity of the individual could assume. This it was which inevitably gave every-day worldly activity a religious significance, and which first created the conception of a calling in this sense. The conception of the calling thus brings out that central dogma of all Protestant denominations which the Catholic division of ethical precepts into *praecepta* and *consilia* discards. The only way of living acceptably to God was not to surpass worldly morality in monastic asceticism, but solely through the fulfillment of the obligations imposed upon the individual by his position in the world. That was his calling.

Luther developed the conception in the course of the first decade of his activity as a reformer. At first, quite in harmony with the prevailing tradition of the Middle Ages, as represented, for example, by Thomas Aquinas he thought of activity in the world as a thing of the flesh, even though willed by God. It is the indispensable natural condition of a life of faith, but in itself, like eating and drinking, morally neutral. But with the development of the conception of *sola fide* in all its consequences, and its logical result, the increasingly sharp emphasis against the Catholic *consilia evangelica* of the monks as dictates of the devil, the calling grew in importance. The monastic life is not only quite devoid of value as a means of justification before God, but he also looks upon its renunciation of the duties of this world as the product of selfishness, withdrawing from temporal obligations. In contrast, labor in a calling appears to him as the outward expression of brotherly love. This he proves by the observation that the division of labor forces every individual to work for others, but his viewpoint is highly naive, forming an almost grotesque contrast to Adam Smith's well known statements on the same subject. However, this justification, which is evidently essentially scholastic, soon disappears again, and there remains, more and more strongly emphasized, the statement that the fulfillment of worldly duties is under all circumstances the only way to live acceptably to God. It and it alone is the will of God, and hence every legitimate calling has exactly the same worth in the sight of God.

That this moral justification of worldly activity was one of the most important results of the Reformation, especially of Luther's part in it, is beyond doubt, and may even be considered a platitude. This attitude is worlds removed from the deep hatred of Pascal, in his contemplative moods, for all worldly activity, which he was deeply convinced could only be understood in terms of vanity or low cunning. And it differs even more from the liberal utilitarian compromise with the world at which the Jesuits arrived. But just what the practical significance of this achievement of Protestantism was in detail is dimly felt rather than clearly perceived.

In the first place it is hardly necessary to point out that Luther cannot be claimed for the spirit of capitalism in the sense in which we have used that term above, or for that matter in any sense whatever. The religious circles which today most enthusiastically celebrate that great achievement of the Reformation are by no means friendly to capitalism in any sense. And Luther himself would, without doubt, have sharply repudiated any connection with a point of view like that of Franklin. Of course, one cannot consider his complaints against the great merchants of his time, such as the Fuggers, as evidence in this case. For the struggle against the privileged position, legal or actual, of single great trading companies in the sixteenth and seventeenth centuries may best be compared with the modem campaign against the trusts, and can no more justly be considered in itself an expression of a traditionalistic point of view. Against these people, against the Lombards, the monopolists, speculators, and bankers patronized by the Anglican Church and the kings and parliaments of England and France, both the Puritans and the Huguenots carried on a bitter struggle. Cromwell, after the battle of Dunbar (September 1650), wrote to the Long Parliament: "Be pleased to reform the abuses of all professions: and if there be any one that makes many poor to make a few rich, that suits not a Commonwealth." But, nevertheless, we will find Cromwell following a quite specifically capitalistic line of thought. On the other hand, Luther's numerous statements against usury or interest in any form reveal a conception of the nature of capitalistic acquisition which, compared with that of late Scholasticism, is, from a capitalistic viewpoint, definitely backward. Especially, of course, the doctrine of the sterility of money which Anthony of Florence had already refuted.

But it is unnecessary to go into detail. For, above all the consequences of the conception of the calling in the religious sense for worldly conduct were susceptible to quite different interpretations. The effect of the Reformation as such was only that, as compared with the Catholic attitude, the moral emphasis on and the religious sanction of, organized worldly labor in a calling was mightily increased. The way in which the concept of the calling, which expressed this change, should develop further depended upon the religious evolution which now took place in the different Protestant Churches. The authority of the Bible, from which Luther thought he had derived his idea of the calling, on the whole favored a traditionalistic interpretation. The old Testament, in particular, though in the genuine prophets it showed no sign of a tendency to excel worldly morality, and elsewhere only in quite isolated rudiments and suggestions, contained a similar religious idea entirely in this traditionalistic sense. Everyone should abide by his living and let the godless run after gain. That is the sense of all the statements which bear directly on worldly activities. Not until the Talmud is a partially, but not even then fundamentally, different attitude to be found. The personal attitude of Jesus is characterized in classical purity by the typical antique Oriental plea: "Give us this day our daily bread." The element of radical repudiation of the world, as expressed in the μαμωνᾶς τῆς ἀδικίας, excluded the possibility that the modern idea of calling should be based on his personal authority. In the apostolic era as expressed in the New Testament, especially in St. Paul, the Christian looked upon worldly activity either with indifference, or at least essentially traditionalistically; for those first generations were filled with eschatological hopes. Since everyone was simply waiting for the coming of the Lord, there was nothing to do but remain in the station and in the worldly occupation in which the call of the Lord had found him, and labor as before. Thus he would not burden his brothers as an object of charity, and it would only be for a little while. Luther read the Bible through the spectacles of his whole attitude; at the time and in the course of his development from about 1518 to 1530 this not only remained traditionalistic but became ever more so.

In the first years of his activity as a reformer he was, since he thought of the calling as primarily of the flesh, dominated by an attitude closely related, in so far as the form of world activity was concerned, to the Pauline eschatological indifference as expressed in I Cor. vii. One may attain salvation in any walk of life; on the short pilgrimage of life there is no use in laying weight on the form of occupation. The pursuit of material gain beyond personal needs must thus appear as a symptom of lack of grace, and since it can apparently only be attained at the expense of others, directly reprehensible. As he became increasingly involved in the affairs of the world, he came to value work in the world more highly. But in the concrete calling an individual pursued he saw more and more a special command of God to fulfill these particular duties which the Divine Will had imposed upon him. And after the conflict with the Fanatics and the peasant disturbances, the objective historical order of things in which the individual has been placed by God becomes for Luther more and more a direct manifestation of divine will. The stronger and stronger emphasis

on the providential element, even in particular events
of life, led more and more to a traditionalistic interpretation based on the idea of Providence. The individual
should remain once and for all in the station and calling
in which God had placed him, and should restrain hi'
worldly activity within the limits imposed by his established station in life. While his economic traditionalism
was originally the result of Pauline indifference, it later became that of a more and more intense belief in divine providence, which identified absolute obedience to
God's will, with absolute acceptance of things as they
were. Starting from this background, it was impossible
for Luther to establish a new or in any way fundamental
connection between worldly activity and religious principles. His acceptance of purity of doctrine as the one
infallible criterion of the Church, which became more
and more irrevocable after the struggles of the twenties,
was in itself sufficient to check the development of new
points of view in ethical matters.

Thus for Luther the concept of the calling remained
traditionalistic. His calling is something which man has
to accept as a divine ordinance, to which he must adapt
himself. This aspect outweighed the other idea which
was also present, that work in the calling was a, or rather
the, task set by God. And in its further development, orthodox Lutheranism emphasized this aspect still more.
Thus, for the time being, the only ethical result was negative; worldly duties were no longer subordinated to
ascetic' ones; obedience to authority and the acceptance
of things as they were, were preached. In this Lutheran
form the idea of a calling had, as will be shown in our
discussion of medieval religious ethics, to a considerable
extent been anticipated by the German mystics. Especially in Tauler's equalization of the values of religious
and worldly occupations, and the decline in valuation
of the traditional forms of ascetic practices on account
of the decisive significance of the ecstatic-contemplative
absorption of the divine spirit by the soul. To a certain
extent Lutheranism means a step backward from the
mystics, in so far as Luther, and still more his Church,

had, as compared with the mystics, partly undermined the psychological foundations for a rational ethics. (The mystic attitude on this point is reminiscent partly of the Pietest and partly of the Quaker psychology of faith.) That was precisely because he could not but suspect the tendency to ascetic self discipline of leading to salvation by works, and hence he and his Church were forced to keep it more and more in the background.

Thus the mere idea of the calling in the Lutheran sense is at best of questionable importance for the problems in which we are interested. This was all that was meant to be determined here. But this is not in the least to say that even the Lutheran form of the renewal of the religious life may not have had some practical significance for the objects of our investigation; quite the contrary. Only that significance evidently cannot be derived directly from the attitude of Luther and his Church to worldly activity, and is perhaps not altogether so easily grasped as the connection with other branches of Protestantism. It is thus well for us next to look into those forms in which a relation between practical life and a religious motivation can be more easily perceived than in Lutheranism. We have already called attention to the conspicuous part played by Calvinism and the Protestant sects in the history of capitalistic development. As Luther found a different spirit at work in Zwingli than in himself, so did his spiritual successors in Calvinism. And Catholicism has to the present day looked upon Calvinism as its real opponent.

Now that may be partly explained on purely political grounds. Although the Reformation is unthinkable without Luther's own personal religious development, and was spiritually long influenced by his personality, without Calvinism his work could not have had permanent concrete success. Nevertheless, the reason for this common repugnance of Catholics and Lutherans lies, at least partly, in the ethical peculiarities of Calvinism. A purely superficial glance shows that there is here quite a different relationship between the religious life and earthly activity than in either Catholicism or Lutheranism. Even in literature motivated purely by religious factors that is evident. Take for instance the end of the *Divine Comedy*, where the poet in Paradise stands speechless in his passive contemplation of the secrets of God, and compare it with the poem which has come to be called the *Divine Comedy of Puritanism*. Milton closes the last song of *Paradise Lost* after describing the expulsion from paradise as follows:-

> "They, looking back, all the eastern side beheld
> Of paradise, so late their happy scat,
> Waved over by that flaming brand; the gate
> With dreadful faces thronged and fiery arms.
> Some natural tears they dropped, but wiped them soon:
> The world was all before them, there to choose
> Their place of rest, and Providence their guide."

And only a little before Michael had said to Adam:

> . . . "Only add
> Deeds to thy knowledge answerable; add faith;
> Add virtue, patience, temperance; add love,
> By name to come called Charity, the soul
> Of all the rest: then wilt thou not be loth
> To leave this Paradise, but shall possess
> A Paradise within thee, happier far."

One feels at once that this powerful expression of the Puritan's serious attention to this world, his acceptance of his life in the world as a task, could not possibly have come from the pen of a medieval writer. But it is just as uncongenial to Lutheranism, as expressed for instance in Luther's and Paul Gerhard's chorales. It is now our task to replace this vague feeling by a somewhat more precise logical formulation, and to investigate the fundamental basis of these differences. The appeal to national character is generally a mere confession of ignorance, and in this case it is entirely untenable. To ascribe a unified national character to the Englishmen of the seventeenth century would be simply to falsify history. Cavaliers and Roundheads did not appeal to each other simply as two parties, but a radically distinct species of men, and whoever look into the matter carefully must agree with them. On the other hand, a difference of character between the English merchant adventurers and the old Hanseatic merchants is not to be found; nor can any other fundamental difference between the English and German characters at the end of the Middle Ages, which cannot easily be explained by the differences of their political history. It was the power of religious influence, not alone, but more than anything else, which created the differences of which we are conscious today.

We thus take as our starting point in the investigation of the relationship between the old Protestant ethic and the spirit of capitalism the works of Calvin, of Calvinism, and the other Puritan sects. But it is not to be understood that we expect to find any of the founders or representatives of these religious movements considering the promotion of what we have called the spirit of capitalism as in any sense the end of his life-work. We cannot well maintain that the pursuit of worldly goods, conceived as an end in itself, was to any of them of positive ethical value. Once and for all it must be remembered that programs of ethical reform never were at the center of interest for any of the religious reformers (among whom, for our purposes, we must include men like Menno, George Fox, and Wesley). They were not the founders of societies for ethical culture nor the proponents of humanitarian projects for social reform or cultural ideals. The salvation of the soul and that alone was the center of their life and work. Their ethical ideals and the practical results of their doctrines were all based on that alone, and were the consequences of purely religious motives. We shall thus have to admit that the cultural consequences of the Reformation were to a great extent, perhaps in the particular aspects with which we are dealing predominantly, unforeseen and even unwished for results of the labors of the reformers. They were often far removed from or even in contradiction to all that they themselves thought to attain.

The following study may thus perhaps in a modest way form a contribution to the understanding of the manner in which ideas become effective forces in history. In order, however, to avoid any misunderstanding of the sense in which any such effectiveness of purely ideal motives is claimed at all, I may perhaps be permitted a few remarks in conclusion to this introductory discussion.

In such a study, it may at once be definitely stated, no attempt is made to evaluate the ideas of the Reformation in any sense, whether it concern their social or their religious worth. We have continually to deal with aspects of the Reformation which must appear to the truly religious consciousness as incidental and even superficial. For we are merely attempting to clarify the part which religious forces have played in forming the developing web of our specifically worldly modern culture, in the complex interaction of innumerable different historical factors. We are thus inquiring only to what extent certain characteristic features of this culture can be imputed to the influence of the Reformation. At the same time we must free ourselves from the idea that it is possible to deduce the Reformation, as a historically necessary result, from certain economic changes. Countless historical circumstances, which cannot be reduced to any economic law, and are not susceptible of economic explanation of any sort, especially purely political processes, had to concur in order that the newly created Churches should survive at all.

On the other hand, however, we have no intention whatever of maintaining such a foolish and doctrinaire thesis as that the spirit of capitalism (in the provisional sense of the term explained above) could only have arisen as the result of certain effects of the Reformation, or even that capitalism as an economic system is a creation of the Reformation. In itself, the fact that certain important forms of capitalistic business organization are known to be considerably older than the Reformation is a sufficient refutation of such a claim On the contrary, we only wish to ascertain whether and to what extent religious forces have taken part in qualitative formation and the quantitative expansion of that spirit over the world. Furthermore, what concrete aspects of our capitalistic culture can be traced to them, In view of the tremendous confusion of interdependent influences between the material basis, the forms of social and political organization, and the ideas current in the time of the Reformation, we can only proceed by investigating whether and at what points certain correlations between forms of religious belief and practical ethics can be worked out. At the same time we shall as far as possible clarify the manner and the general *direction* in which, by virtue of those relationships, the religious movements have influenced the development of material culture. Only when this has been determined with reasonable accuracy can the attempt be made to estimate to what extent the historical development of modern culture can be attributed to those religious forces and to what extent to others.

PART II:
THE PRACTICAL ETHICS OF THE ASCETIC BRANCHES OF PROTESTANTISM

Chapter IV.

THE RELIGIOUS FOUNDATIONS OF WORLDLY ASCETICISM

In history there have been four principal forms of ascetic Protestantism (in the sense of word here used): (1) Calvinism in the form which it assumed in the main area of its influence in Western Europe, especially in the seventeenth century; (2) Pietism; (3) Methodism; (4) the sects growing out of the Baptist movement. None of these movements was completely separated from the others, and even the distinction from the non-ascetic Churches of the Reformation is never perfectly clear. Methodism, which first arose in the middle of the eighteenth century within the Established Church of England, was not, in the, minds of its founders, intended to form a new Church, but only a new awakening of the ascetic spirit within the old. Only in the course of its development, especially in its extension to America, did it become separate from the Anglican Church.

Pietism first split off from the Calvinistic movement in England, and especially in Holland. It remained loosely connected with orthodoxy, shading off from it by imperceptible gradations, until at the end of the seventeenth century it was absorbed into Lutheranism under Spener's leadership. Though the dogmatic adjustment was not entirely satisfactory, it remained a movement within the Lutheran Church. Only the faction dominated by Zinzendorf, and affected by lingering Hussite and Calvinistic influences within the Moravian brotherhood, was forced, like Methodism against its will, to form a peculiar sort of sect. Calvinism and Baptism were at the beginning of their development sharply opposed to each other. But in the Baptism of the latter part of the seventeenth century they were in close contact. And, even in the Independent sects of England and Holland at the beginning of the seventeenth century the transition was not abrupt. As Pietism shows, the transition to Lutheranism is also gradual, and the same is true of Calvinism and the Anglican Church, though both in external character and in the spirit of its most logical adherents the latter is more closely related to Catholicism. It is true that both the mass of the adherents and especially the staunchest champions of that ascetic movement which, in the broadest sense of a highly ambiguous word, has been called Puritanism, did attack the foundations of Anglicanism; but even here the differences were only gradually worked out in the course of the struggle. Even if for the present we quite ignore the questions, of government and organization which do not interest us here, the facts are just the same. The dogmatic differences, even the most important, such as those over the doctrines of predestination and justification, were combined in the most complex ways, and even at the beginning of the seventeenth century regularly, though not without exception, prevented the maintenance o unity in the Church. Above all, the types of moral conduct in which we are interested may be found in similar manner among the adherents of the most various denominations, derived from any one of the four sources mentioned above, or a combination of several of them. We shall see that similar ethical maxims may be correlated with very different dogmatic foundations. Also the important literary tools for the saving of souls, above all the casuistic compendia of the various denominations, influenced each other in the course of time; one finds great similarities in them, in spite of very great differences in actual conduct.

It would almost seem as though we had best completely ignore both the dogmatic foundations and the ethical theory and confine our attention to the moral

practice so far as it can be determined. That, however, is
not true. The various different dogmatic roots of ascetic morality did no doubt die out after terrible struggles.
But the original connection with those dogmas has left
behind important traces in the later undogmatic ethics;
moreover, only the knowledge of the original body of
ideas can help us to understand the connection of that
morality with the idea of the after-life which absolutely
dominated the most spiritual men of that time. Without its power, overshadowing everything else, no moral awakening which seriously influenced practical life
came into being in that period.

We are naturally not concerned with the question
of what was theoretically and officially taught in the
ethical compendia of the time, however much practical
significance this may have had through the influence of
Church discipline, pastoral work, and preaching. We are
interested rather in something entirely different: the influence of those psychological sanctions which, originat-
ing in religious belief and the practice of religion, gave
a direction to practical conduct and held the individual
to it. Now these sanctions were to a large extent derived
from the peculiarities of the religious ideas behind them.
The men of that day were occupied with abstract dogmas to an extent which itself can only be understood
when we perceive the connection of these dogmas with
practical religious interests. A few observations on dogma, which will seem to the non-theological reader as
dull as they will hasty and superficial to the theologian,
are indispensable. We can of course only proceed by pre-
senting these religious ideas in the artificial simplicity of
ideal types, as they could at best but seldom be found in
history. For just because of the impossibility of drawing
sharp boundaries in historical reality we can only hope
to understand their specific importance from an investigation of them in their most consistent and logical forms.

A. Calvinism

Now Calvinism was the faith over which the great political and cultural struggles of the sixteenth and sev-

enteenth centuries were fought in the most highly developed countries, the Netherlands, England, and France. To it we shall hence turn first. At that time, and in general even today, the doctrine of predestination was considered its most characteristic dogma. It is true that there has been controversy as to whether it is the most essential dogma of the Reformed Church or only an appendage. Judgments of the importance of a historical phenomenon may be judgments of value or faith, namely, when they refer to what is. alone interesting, or alone in the long run valuable in it. Or, on the other hand, they may refer to its influence on other historical processes as a causal factor. Then we are concerned with judgments o historical imputation. If now we start, as we must do here, from the latter standpoint and inquire into the significance which is to be attributed to that dogma by virtue Of its cultural and historical con sequences, it must certainly be rated very highly. The movement which Oldenbameveld led was shattered by it. The schism in the English Church became irrevocable under James I after the Crown and the Puritans came to differ dogmatically over just this doctrine. Again and again it was looked upon as the real element of political danger in Calvinism and attacked as such by those in authority. The great synods of the seventeenth century, above all those of Dordrecht and Westminster, besides numerous smaller ones, made its elevation to canonical authority the central purpose of their work. It served as a rallying point to countless heroes of the Church militant, and in both the eighteenth and the nineteenth centuries it caused schisms in the Church and formed the battle cry of great new awakenings. We cannot pass it by, and since today it can no longer be assumed as known to all educated men, we can best learn its content from the authoritative words of the Westminster Confession of 1647, which in this regard is simply repeated by both Independent and Baptist creeds.

"Chapter IX (of Free Will), No. 3- Man, by his fall into a state of sin, hath wholly lost all ability of will to any spiritual good accompanying salvation. So that a natural man, being altogether averse from that Good, and dead in sin, is not able, by his own strength, to convert himself, or to prepare himself thereunto.

"Chapter III (of God's Eternal Decree), No. 3. By the decree of God, for the manifestation of His glory, some men and angels are predestinated unto ever-lasting life, and others foreordained to everlasting death.

"No. 5. Those of mankind that are predestinated unto life, God before the foundation of the world was laid, according to His eternal and immutable purpose, and the secret counsel and good pleasure of His will, hath chosen in Christ unto everlasting glory, out of His mere free grace and love, without any foresight of faith or good works, or perseverance in either of them, or any other thing in the creature as conditions, or causes moving Him thereunto, and all to the praise of His glorious grace.

"No. 7. The rest of mankind God was pleased, according to the unsearchable counsel of His own will, whereby He extendeth, or with-holdeth mercy, as He pleaseth, for the glory of His sovereign power over His creatures, to pass by, and to ordain them to dishonour and wrath for their sin, to the praise of His glorious justice.

"Chapter X (of Effectual Calling), No. 1. All those whom God hath predestinated unto life, and those only, He is pleased in His appointed and accepted time effectually to call, by His word and spirit (out of that state of sin and death, in which they are by nature)...taking away their heart of stone, and giving unto them an heart of flesh; renewing their wills, and by His almighty power determining them to that which is good...

"Chapter V (of Providence), No. 6. As for those wicked and ungodly men, whom God as a righteous judge, for former sins doth blind and harden, from them He not only withholdeth His grace, whereby they might have been enlightened in their understandings and wrought upon in their hearts, but sometimes also withdraweth the gifts which they had and exposeth them to such objects as their corruption makes occasion of sin: and with-al, gives them over to their own lusts, the temptations of the world, and the power of Satan: whereby it comes to pass that they harden themselves, even under those means, which God useth for the softening of others."

"Though I may be sent to Hell for it, such a God will never command my respect", was Milton's well known opinion of the doctrine. But we are here concerned not with the evaluation, but the historical significance of the dogma. We can only briefly sketch the question of how the doctrine originated and how it fitted into the frame-work of Calvinistic theology.

Two paths leading to it were possible. The phenom-enon of the religious sense of grace is combined, in the most active and passionate of those great worshippers which Christianity has produced again and again since Augustine, with the feeling of certainty that that grace is the sole product of an objective power, and not in the least to be attributed to personal worth. The powerful feeling of light-hearted assurance, in which the tremen-dous pressure of their sense of sin is released, apparent-ly breaks over them with elemental force and destroys every possibility of the belief that this overpowering gift of grace could owe anything to their own cooperation or could be connected with achievements or qualities of their own faith and will. At the time of Luther's greatest religious creativeness, when he was capable of writing his *Freiheit eines Christenmenschen*, God's secret decree was also to him most definitely the sole and ultimate source of his state of religious grace. Even later he did not formally abandon it. But not only did the idea not assume a central position for him, but it receded more and more into the back-ground, the more his position as responsible head of his Church forced him into practical politics. Melancthon quite deliberately avoided adopt-ing the dark and dangerous teaching in the Augsburg Confession, and for the Church fathers of Lutheranism it was an article of faith that grace was revocable (*amissi-bilis*), and could be won again by penitent humility and faithful trust in the word of God and in the sacraments.

With Calvin the process was just the opposite; the significance of the doctrine for him increased, perceptibly in the course of his polemical controversies with theological opponents. It is not fully developed until the third edition of his *Institutes*, and only gained its position of central prominence after his death in the great struggles which the Synods of Dordrecht and Westminster sought to put an end to. With Calvin the *decretum horribile* is derived not, as with Luther, from religious experience, but from the logical necessity of his thought; -therefore its importance increases with every increase in the logical consistency of that religious thought. The interest of it is solely in God, not in man; God does not exist for men, but men for the sake of God. All creation, including of course the fact, as it undoubtedly was for Calvin, that only a small pro-portion of men are chosen for eternal grace, can have any meaning only as means to the glory and majesty of God. To apply earthly standards of justice to His sovereign decrees is meaningless and an insult to His Majesty, since He and He alone is free, i.e. is subject to no law. His decrees can only be understood by or even known to us in so far as it has been His pleasure to reveal them. We can only hold to these fragments of eternal truth. Everything else, including the meaning of our individual destiny, is hidden in dark mystery which it would be both impossible to pierce and presumptuous to question.

For the damned to complain of their lot would be much the same as for animals to bemoan the fact they were not born as men. For everything of the flesh is separated from God by an unbridgeable gulf and deserves of Him only eternal death, in so far as He has not decreed otherwise for the glorification of His Majesty. We know only that a part of humanity is saved, the rest damned. To assume that human merit or guilt play a part in determining this destiny would be to think of God's absolutely free decrees, which have been settled from eternity, as subject to change by human influence, an impossible contradiction. The Father in heaven of the New Testament, so human and under-standing, who rejoices over the repentance of a sinner as a woman over the lost piece of silver she has found, is gone. His place has been taken by a transcendental being, beyond the reach of human understanding, who with His quite incomprehensible decrees has decided the fate of every individual and regulated the tiniest details of the cosmos from eternity. God's grace is, since His decrees cannot change, as impossible for those to whom He has granted it to lose as it is unattainable for those to whom He has denied it.

In its extreme inhumanity this doctrine must above all have had one consequence for the life of a generation which surrendered to its magnificent consistency. That was a feeling of unprecedented inner loneliness of the single individual. In what was for the man of the age of the Reformation the most important thing in life, his eternal salvation, he was forced to follow his path alone to meet a destiny which had been decreed for him from eternity. No one could help him. No priest, for the chosen one can understand the word of God only in his own heart. No sacraments, for though the sacraments had been ordained by God for the increase of His glory, and must hence be scrupulously observed, they are not a means to the attainment of grace, but only the subjective *externa subsidia* of faith. No Church, for though it was held that *extra ecclesiam nulla salus* in the sense that whoever kept away from the true Church could never belong to God's chosen band, nevertheless the membership of the external Church included the doomed. They should belong to it and be subjected to its discipline, not in order thus to attain salvation, that is impossible, but because, for the glory of God, they too must be forced to obey His commandments. Finally, even no God. For even Christ had died only for the elect, for whose benefit God had decreed His martyrdom from eternity. This, the complete elimination of salvation through the Church and the sacraments (which was in Lutheranism by no means developed to its final conclusions), was what formed the absolutely decisive difference from Catholicism.

That great historic process in the development of religions, the elimination of magic from the world which had begun with the old Hebrew prophets and, in conjunction with Hellenistic scientific thought, had repudiated all magical means to salvation as superstition and sin, came here to its logical conclusion. The genuine Puritan even rejected all signs of religious ceremony at the grave and buried his nearest and dearest without song or ritual in order that no superstition, no trust in the effects of magical and sacramental forces on salvation, should creep in.

There was not only no magical means of attaining the grace of God for those to whom God had decided to deny it, but no means whatever. Combined with the harsh doctrines of the absolute transcendentiality of God and the corruption of everything pertaining to the flesh, this inner isolation of the individual contains, on the one hand, the reason for the entirely negative attitude of Puritanism to all the sensuous and emotional elements in culture and in religion, because they are of no use toward salvation and promote sentimental illusions and idolatrous superstitions. Thus it provides a basis for a fundamental antagonism to sensuous culture of all kinds. On the other hand, it forms one of the roots of that disillusioned and pessimistically inclined individualism which can even today be identified in the national characters and the institutions of the peoples with a Puritan past, in such a striking contrast to the quite different spectacles through which the Enlightenment later looked upon men. We can clearly identify the traces of the influence of the doctrine of predestination in the elementary forms of conduct and attitude toward life in the era with which we are concerned, even where its authority as a dogma was on the decline. It was in fact only the most extreme form of that exclusive trust in God in which we are here interested. It comes out for instance in the strikingly frequent repetition, especially in the English Puritan literature, of warnings against any trust in the aid of friendship of men. Even the amiable Baxter counsels deep distrust of even one's closest friend, and Bailey directly exhorts to trust no one and to say nothing compromising to anyone. Only God should be your confidant. In striking contrast to Lutheranism, this attitude toward life was also connected with the quiet disappearance of the private confession, of which Calvin was suspicious only on account of its possible sacramental misinterpretation, from all the regions of fully developed Calvinism. That was an occurrence of the greatest importance. In the first place it is a symptom of the type of influence this religion exercised. Further, however, it was a psychological stimulus to the development Of their ethical attitude. The means to a periodical discharge of the emotional sense of sin was done away with.

Of the consequences for the ethical conduct of everyday life we speak later. But for the general religious situation of a man the consequences are evident. In spite of the necessity of membership in the true Church for salvation, the Calvinist's intercourse with his God was carried on in deep spiritual isolation. To see the specific results of this peculiar atmosphere, it is only necessary to read Bunyan's, *Pilgrim's Progress,* by far the most widely read book of the whole Puritan literature. In the description of Christian's attitude after he had realized that he was living in the City of Destruction and he had received the call to take tip his pilgrim-age to the celestial city, wife and children cling to him, but stopping his ears with his fingers and crying, "life, eternal life", he staggers forth across the fields. No refinement could surpass the naive feeling of the tinker who, writing in his prison cell, earned the applause of a believing world, in expressing the emotions of the faithful Puritan, thinking only of his own salvation. It is expressed in the unctuous conversations which he holds with fellow-seekers on the way, in a manner somewhat reminiscent of Gottfried Keller's *Gerechte Kammacher*. Only when he himself is safe does it occur to him that it would be nice to have his family with him. It is the same anxious fear of death and the beyond which we feel so vividly in Alfonso of Liguori, as Dollinger has described him to us. It is worlds removed from that spirit of proud worldliness which Machiavelli expresses in relating the fame of those Florentine citizens who, in their struggle against the Pope and his excommunication, had held "Love of their native city higher than the fear for the salvation of their souls". And it is of course even farther from the feelings which Richard Wagner puts into the mouth of Siegmund before his fatal combat, "Grusse mir Wotan, grusse mir Wallhall-Doch von Wallhall's sproden Wonnen sprich du wahrlich mir nicht". But the effects of this fear on Bunyan and Liguori are characteristically different. The same fear which drives the latter to every conceivable self humiliation spurs the former on to a restless and systematic struggle with life. Whence comes this difference?

It seems at first a mystery how the undoubted superiority of Calvinism in social organization can be connected with this tendency to tear the individual away from the closed ties with which he is bound to this world. But, however strange it may seem, it follows from the peculiar form which the Christian brotherly love was forced to take under the pressure of the inner isolation of the individual through the Calvinistic faith. In the first place it follows dogmatically. The world exists to serve the glorification of God and for that purpose alone. The elected Christian is in the world only to increase this glory of God by fulfilling His commandments to the best of his ability. But God requires social achievement of the Christian because He wills that social life shall be organized according to His commandments, in accordance with that purpose. The social activity of the Christian in the world is' solely activity *in majorem gloriam Dei.* This character is hence shared by labor in a calling which serves the mundane life of the community. Even in Luther we found specialized labor in callings justified in terms of brotherly love. But what for him remained an un-certain, purely intellectual suggestion became for the Calvinists a characteristic element in their ethical system. Brotherly love, since it may only be practiced for the glory of God and not in the service of the flesh, is expressed in the first place in the fulfillment of the daily tasks given by the *lex naturae*; and in the Process this fulfillment assumes a peculiarly objective and impersonal character, that of service in the interest of the rational organization of our social environment. For the wonderfully purposeful organization and arrangement of this cosmos is, according both to the revelation of the Bible and to natural intuition, evidently designed by God to serve the utility of the human race. This makes labor in the service of impersonal social usefulness appear to promote the glory of God and hence to he willed by Him. The complete elimination of the theodicy problem and of all those questions about the meaning of the world and of life, which have tortured others, was as self-evident to the Puritan as, for quite different reasons, to the Jew, and even in a certain sense to all the non mystical types of Christian religion.

To this economy of forces Calvinism added another tendency which worked in the same direction. The conflict between the individual and the ethic (in Soren Kierkegaard's sense) did not exist for Calvinism, although it placed the individual entirely on his own responsibility in religious matters. This is not the place to analyze the reasons for this fact, or its significance for the political and economic rationalism of Calvinism. The source of the utilitarian character of Calvinistic ethics lies here, and important peculiarities of the Calvinistic idea of the calling were derived from the same source as well. But for the moment we must return to the special consideration of the doctrine of predestination.

For us the decisive problem is: How was this doctrine borne in an age to which the after-life was not only more important, but in many ways also more certain, than all the interests of life in this world ? The question, Am I one of the elect? must sooner or later have arisen for every believer and have forced all other interests into the background. And how can I be sure of this state of grace? For Calvin himself this was not a problem. He felt himself to be a chosen agent of the Lord, and was certain of his own salvation. Accordingly, to the question of how the individual can be certain of his own election, he has at bottom only the answer that we should be content with the knowledge that God has chosen and depend further only on that implicit trust in Christ which is the result of true faith. He rejects in principle the assumption that one can learn from the conduct of others whether they are chosen or damned. It is an unjustifiable attempt to force God's secrets. The elect differ externally in this life in no way from the damned; and even all the subjective experiences of the chosen are, as *ludibria spiritus sancti,* possible for the damned with the single exception of that *finaliter* expectant, trusting faith. The elect thus are and remain God's invisible Church.

Quite naturally this attitude was impossible for his followers as early as Beza, and, above all, for the broad mass of ordinary men. For them the *certitudo salutis* in the sense of the recognizability of the state of grace necessarily became of absolutely dominant importance. So, wherever the doctrine of predestination was held, the question could not be suppressed whether there were any infallible criteria by which membership in the *electi* could be known. Not only has this question continually had a central importance in the development of the Pietism which first arose on the basis of the Reformed Church; it has in fact in a certain sense at times been fundamental to it. But when we consider the great political and social importance of the Reformed doctrine and practice of the Communion, we shall see how great a part was played during the whole seventeenth century outside of Pietism by the possibility of ascertaining the state of grace of the individual. On it depended, for instance, his admission to Communion, i.e. to the central religious ceremony which determined the social standing of the participants.

It was impossible, at least so far as the question of a man's own state of grace arose, to be satisfied with Calvin's trust in the testimony of the expectant faith resulting from grace, even though the orthodox doctrine had never formally abandoned that criterion." Above all, practical pastoral work, which had immediately to deal with all the suffering caused by the doctrine, could not be satisfied. It met these difficulties in various ways. So far as predestination was not reinterpreted, toned down, or fundamentally abandoned, two principal, mutually connected, types of pastoral advice appear. On the one hand it is held to be an absolute duty to consider oneself chosen, and to combat all doubts as temptations of the devil, since lack of self-confidence is the result of insufficient faith, hence of imperfect grace. The exhortation of the apostle to make fast one's own call is here interpreted as a duty to attain certainty of one's own election and justification in the daily struggle of life. In the place of the humble sinners to whom Luther promises grace if they trust themselves to God in penitent faith are bred those self-confident saints whom we can rediscover in the hard Puritan merchants of the heroic age of capitalism and in isolated instances down to the present. On the other hand, in order to attain that self-confidence intense worldly activity is recommended as the most suitable means. It and it alone disperses religious doubts and gives the certainty of grace.

That worldly activity should be considered capable of this achievement, that it could, so to speak, be considered the most suitable means of counteracting feelings of religious anxiety, finds its explanation in the fundamental peculiarities of religious feeling in the Reformed Church, which come most clearly to light in its differences from Lutheranism in the doctrine of justification by faith. These differences are analyzed so subtly and with such objectivity and avoidance of value judgments in Schneckenburger's excellent lectures, that the following brief observations can for the most part simply rest upon his discussion.

The highest religious experience which the Lutheran faith strives to attain, especially as it developed in the course of the seventeenth century, is the *unio mystica* with the deity. As the name itself, which is unknown to the Reformed faith in this form, suggests, it is a feeling of actual absorption in the deity, that of a real entrance of the divine into the soul of the believer. It is qualitatively similar to the aim of the contemplation of the German mystics and is characterized by its passive search for the fulfillment of the yearning for rest in God.

Now the history of philosophy shows that religious belief which is primarily mystical may very well be compatible with a pronounced sense of reality in the field of empirical fact; it may even support it directly on account of the repudiation of dialectic doctrines. Furthermore, mysticism may indirectly even further the interests of rational conduct. Nevertheless, the positive valuation of external activity is lacking in its relation to the world. In addition to this, Lutheranism combines the *unio mystica* with that deep feeling of sin-stained unworthiness which is essential to preserve the *poenitentia quotidiana* of the faithful Lutheran, thereby maintaining the humility and simplicity in-dispensable for the forgiveness of sins. The typical religion of the Reformed Church, on the other hand, has from the beginning repudiated both this purely inward emotional piety of Lutheranism and the Quietist escape from everything of Pascal. A real penetration of the human soul by the divine was made impossible by the absolute transcendentiality of God compared to the flesh: *finitum non est capax infiniti*. The community of the elect with their God could only take place and be perceptible to them in that God worked (*operatur*) through them and that they were conscious of it. That is, their action originated from the faith caused by God's grace, and this faith in turn justified itself by the quality of that action. Deep lying differences of the most important conditions of salvation" which apply to the classification of all practical religious activity appear here. The religious believer can make himself sure of his state of grace either in that he feels himself to be the vessel of the Holy Spirit or the tool of the divine will. In the former case his religious life tends to mysticism and emotionalism, in the latter to ascetic action; Luther stood close to the former type, Calvinism belonged definitely to the latter. The Calvinist also wanted to be saved *sola fide*. But since Calvin viewed all pure feelings and emotions, no matter how exalted they might seem to be, with suspicion, faith had to be proved by its objective results in order to provide a firm foundation for the *certitudo salutis*. It must be a *fides efficax*, the call to salvation an effectual calling (expression used in Savoy Declaration).

If we now ask further, by what fruits the Calvinist thought himself able to identify true faith? the answer is: by a type of Christian conduct which served to increase the glory of God. just what does so serve is to be seen in his own will as revealed either directly through the Bible or indirectly through the purposeful order of the world which he has created (*lex naturae*). Especially by comparing the condition of one's own soul with that of the elect, for instance the patriarchs, according to the Bible, could the state of one's own grace be known. Only one of the elect really has the *fides efficax*, only he is able by virtue of his rebirth (*regeneratio*) and the resulting sanctification (*sanctificatio*) of his whole life, to augment the glory of God by real, and not merely apparent, good works. It was through the consciousness that his conduct, at least in its fundamental character and constant ideal (*propositum obaedientiae*), rested on a power" within himself working for the glory of God; that it is not only willed of God but rather done by God that he attained the highest good towards which this religion strove, the certainty of salvation. That it was attainable was proved by 2 Cor. xiii. 5. Thus, however useless good works might be as a means of attaining salvation, for even the elect remain beings of the flesh, and everything they do falls infinitely short of divine standards, nevertheless, they are indispensable as a sign of election". They are the technical means, not of purchasing salvation, but of getting rid of the fear of damnation. In this sense they are occasionally referred to as directly necessary for salvation or the *possessio salutis* is made conditional on them.

In practice this means that God helps those who help themselves. Thus the Calvinist, as it is sometimes put, himself creates his own salvation, or, as would be more correct, the conviction of it. But this creation cannot, as in Catholicism, consist in a gradual accumulation of individual good works to one's credit, but rather in a systematic self-control which at every moment stands before the inexorable alternative, chosen or damned.

This brings us to a very important point in our investigation. It is common knowledge that Lutherans have again and again accused this line of thought, which was worked out in the Reformed Churches and sects with increasing clarity, of reversion to the doctrine of salvation by works. And however justified the protest of the accused against identification of their dogmatic position with the Catholic doctrine, this accusation has surely been made with reason if by it is meant the practical consequences for the everyday life of the average Christian of the Reformed Church." For a more intensive form of the religious valuation of moral action than that to which Calvinism led its adherents has perhaps never existed. But what is important for the practical significance of this sort of salvation by works must be sought in a knowledge of the particular qualities which characterized their type of ethical conduct and distinguished it from the everyday life of an average Christian of the Middle Ages. The difference may well be formulated as follows: the normal medieval Catholic layman lived ethically, so to speak, from hand to mouth. In the first place he conscientiously fulfilled his traditional duties. But beyond that minimum his good works did not necessarily form a connected, or at least not a rationalized, system of life, but rather remained a succession of individual acts. He could use them as occasion demanded, to atone for particular sins, to better his chances for salvation, or, toward the end of his life, as a sort of insurance premium. Of course the Catholic ethic was an ethic of intentions. But the concrete *intentio* of the single act determined its value. And the single good or bad action was credited to the doer determining his temporal and eternal fate. Quite realistically the Church recognized that man was not an absolutely clearly defined unity to be judged one way or the other, but that his moral life was normally subject to conflicting motives and his action contradictory. Of course, it required as an ideal a change of life in principle. But it weakened just this requirement (for the average) by one of its most important means of power and education, the sacrament of absolution, the function of which was connected with the deepest roots of the peculiarly Catholic religion.

The rationalization of the world, the elimination of magic as a means to salvation, the Catholics had not carried nearly so far as the Puritans (and before them the Jews) had done. To the Catholics the absolution of his Church was a compensation for his own imperfection. The priest was a magician who performed the miracle of transubstantiation, and who held the key to eternal life in his hand. One could turn to him in grief and penitence. He dispensed atonement, hope of grace, certainty of forgiveness, and thereby granted release from that tremendous tension to which the Calvinist was doomed by an inexorable fate, admitting of no mitigation. For him such friendly and human comforts did not exist. He could not hope to atone for hours of weakness or of thoughtlessness by increased good will at other times, as the Catholic or even the Lutheran could. The God of Calvinism demanded of his believers not single good works, but a life of good works combined into a unified system." There was no place for the very human Catholic cycle of sin, repentance, atonement, release, followed by renewed sin. Nor was there any balance of merit for a life as a whole which could be adjusted by temporal punishments or the Churches' means of grace.

The moral conduct of the average man was thus deprived of its planless and unsystematic character and subjected to a consistent method for conduct as a whole. It is no accident that the name of Methodists stuck to the participants in the last great revival of Puritan ideas in the eighteenth century just as the term Precisians, which has the same meaning, was applied to their spiritual ancestors in the seventeenth century. For only by a fundamental change in the whole meaning of life at every moment and in every action could the effects of grace transforming a man from the *status naturae*, to the *status gratiae* be proved.

The life of the saint was directed solely toward a transcendental end, salvation. But precisely for that reason it was thoroughly rationalized in this world and dominated entirely by the aim to add to the glory of God on earth. Never has the precept *omnia in majorem dei gloriam* been taken with more bitter seriousness. Only a life guided by constant thought could achieve conquest over the state of nature. Descartes's *cogito ergo sum* was taken over by the contemporary Puritans with this ethical reinterpretation. It was this rationalization which gave the Reformed faith its peculiar ascetic tendency, and is the basis both of its relationship to and its conflict with Catholicism. For naturally similar things were not unknown to Catholicism.

Without doubt Christian asceticism, both outwardly and in its inner meaning, contains many different things. But it has had a definitely rational character in its highest Occidental forms as early as the Middle Ages, and in several forms even in antiquity. The great historical significance of Western monasticism, as contrasted with that of the Orient, is based on this fact, not in all cases, but in its general type. In the rules of St. Benedict, still more with the monks of Cluny, again with the Cistercians, and most strongly the Jesuits, it has become emancipated from planless otherworldliness and irrational self-torture. It had developed a systematic method of rational conduct with the purpose of overcoming the *status naturae*, to free man from the power of irrational impulses and his dependence on the world and on nature. It attempted to subject man to the supremacy of a purposeful will, to bring his actions under constant self-control with a careful consideration of their ethical consequences. Thus it trained the monk, objectively, as a worker in the service of the kingdom of God, and thereby further, subjectively, assured the salvation of his soul. This active self-control, which formed the end of the *exercitia* of St. Ignatius and of the rational monastic virtues everywhere was also the most important practical ideal of Puritanism. In the deep contempt with which the cool reserve of its adherents is contrasted, in the reports of the trials of its martyrs, with the undisciplined blustering of the noble prelates and officials can be seen that respect for quiet self-control which still distinguishes the best type of English or American gentleman today. To put it in our terms: The Puritan, like every rational type of asceticism, tried to enable a man to maintain and act upon his constant motives, especially those which it g in itself, against the emotions. In this formal psychological sense of the term it tried to make him into a personality. Contrary to many popular ideas, the end of this asceticism was to be able to lead an alert, intelligent life: the most urgent task the destruction of spontaneous, impulsive enjoyment, the most important means was to bring order into the conduct of its adherents. All these important points are emphasized in the rules of Catholic monasticism as strongly as in the principles of conduct of the Calvinists." On this methodical control over the whole man rests the enormous expansive power of both, especially the ability of Calvinism as against Lutheranism to defend the cause of Protestantism as the Church militant.

On the other hand, the difference of the Calvinistic from the medieval asceticism is evident. It consisted in the disappearance of the *consilia evangelica* and the accompanying transformation of asceticism to activity within the world. It is not as though Catholicism had restricted the methodical life to monastic cells. This was by no means the case either in theory or in practice. On the contrary, it has already been pointed out that, in spite of the greater ethical moderation of Catholicism, an ethically unsystematic life did not satisfy the highest ideals which it had set up even for the life of the layman. The tertiary order of St. Francis was, for instance, a powerful attempt in the direction of an ascetic penetration of everyday life, and, as we know, by no means the only one. But, in fact, works like the *Nachfolge Christi* show, through the manner in which their strong influence was exerted, that the way of life preached in them was felt to be something higher than the everyday morality which sufficed as a minimum, and that this latter was not measured by such standards as Puritanism demanded. Moreover, the practical use made of certain institutions of the Church, above all of indulgences inevitably counteracted the tendencies toward systematic worldly asceticism. For that reason it was not felt at the time of the Reformation to be merely an unessential abuse, but one of the most fundamental evils of the Church.

But the most important thing was the fact that the man who, *par excellence,* lived a rational life in the religious sense was, and remained, alone the monk. Thus asceticism, the more strongly it gripped an individual, simply served to drive him farther away from everyday life, because the holiest task was definitely to surpass all worldly morality.' Luther, who was not in any sense fulfilling any law of development, but acting upon his quite personal experience, which was, though at first somewhat uncertain in its practical consequences, later pushed farther by the political situation, had repudiated that tendency, and Calvinism simply took this over from him. Sebastian Franck struck the central characteristic of this type of religion when he saw the significance of the Reformation in the fact that now every Christian had to be a monk all his life. The drain of asceticism from everyday worldly life had been stopped by a dam, and those passionately spiritual natures which had formerly supplied the highest type of monk were now forced to pursue their ascetic ideals within mundane occupations.

But in the course of its development Calvinism added something positive to this, the idea of the necessity of proving one's faith in worldly activity. Therein it gave the broader groups of religiously inclined people a positive incentive to asceticism. By founding its ethic in the doctrine of predestination, it substituted for the spiritual aristocracy of monks outside of and above the world the spiritual aristocracy of the predestined saints of God within the world. It was an aristocracy which, with its *character indelebilis*, was divided from the eternally damned remainder of humanity by a more impassable and in its invisibility more terrifying gulf, than separated the monk of the Middle Ages from the rest of the world about him, a gulf which penetrated all social relations with its sharp brutality. This consciousness of divine grace of the elect and holy was accompanied by an attitude toward the sin of one's neighbour, not of sympathetic understanding based on consciousness of one's own weakness, but of hatred and contempt for him as an enemy of God bearing the signs of eternal damnation. This sort of feeling was capable of such intensity that it sometimes resulted in the formation of sects. This was the case when, as in the Independent movement of the seventeenth century, the genuine Calvinist doctrine that the glory of God required the Church to bring the damned under the law, was outweighed by the conviction that it was an insult to God if an unregenerate soul should be admitted to His house and partake in the sacraments, or even, as a minister, administer them. Thus, as a consequence of the doctrine of proof, the Donatist idea of the Church appeared, as in the case of the Calvinistic Baptists. The full logical consequence of the demand for a pure Church, a community of those proved to be in a state of grace, was not often drawn by forming sects. Modifications in the constitution of the Church resulted from the attempt to separate regenerate from unregenerate Christians, those who were from those who were not prepared for the sacrament, to keep the government of the Church or some other privilege in the hands of the former, and only to ordain ministers of whom there was no question.

The norm by which it could always measure itself, of which it was evidently in need, this asceticism naturally found in the Bible. It is important to note that the well-known bibliocracy of the Calvinists held the moral precepts of the Old Testament, since it was fully as authentically revealed, on the same level of esteem as those of the New. It was only necessary that they should not obviously be applicable only to the historical circumstances of the Hebrews, or have been specifically denied by Christ. For the believer, the law was an ideal though never quite attainable normal while Luther, on the other hand, originally had prized freedom from subjugation to the law as a divine privilege of the believer. The influence of the God-fearing but perfectly unemotional wisdom of the Hebrews, which is expressed in the books most read by the Puritans, the Proverbs and the Psalms, can be felt in their whole attitude toward life. In particular, its rational suppression of the mystical, in fact the whole emotional side of religion, has rightly been attributed by Sanford to the influence of the Old Testament. But this Old Testament rationalism was as such essentially of a small bourgeois, traditionalistic type, and was mixed not only with the powerful pathos of the prophets, but also with elements which encouraged the development of a peculiarly emotional type of religion even in the Middle Ages. It was thus in the last analysis the peculiar, fundamentally ascetic, character of Calvinism itself which made it select and assimilate those elements of Old Testament religion which suited it best.

Now that systematization of ethical conduct which the asceticism of Calvinistic Protestantism had in common with the rational forms of life in the Catholic orders is expressed quite superficially in the way in which the conscientious Puritan continually super-vised his own state of grace. To be sure, the religious account-books in which sins, temptations, and progress made in grace were entered or tabulated were common to both the most enthusiastic Reformed circle and some parts of modern Catholicism (especially in France), above all under the influence of the Jesuits. But in Catholicism it served the purpose of completeness of the confession, or gave the *directeur de l'ame* a basis for his authoritarian guidance of the Christian (mostly female). The Reformed Christian, however, felt his own pulse with its aid. It is mentioned by all the moralists and theologians, while Benjamin Franklin's tabulated statistical book-keeping on his progress in the different virtues is a classic example.

On the other hand, the old medieval (even ancient) idea of God's book-keeping is carried by Bunyan to the characteristically tasteless extreme of comparing the relation of a sinner to his God with that of customer and shopkeeper. One who has once got into debt may well, by the product of all his virtuous acts, succeed in paying off the accumulated interest but never the principal. As he observed his own conduct, the later Puritan also observed that of God and saw His finger in all the details of life. And, contrary to the strict doctrine of Calvin, he always knew why God took this or that measure. The process of sanctifying life could thus almost take on the character of a business enterprise. A thoroughgoing Christianization of the whole of life was the consequence of this methodical quality of ethical conduct into which Calvinism as distinct from Lutheranism forced men. That this rationality was decisive in its influence on practical life must always be borne in mind in order rightly to understand the influence of Calvinism. On the one hand we can see that it took this element to exercise such an influence at all. But other faiths as well necessarily bad a similar influence when their ethical motives were the same in this decisive point, the doctrine of proof.

So far we have considered only Calvinism, and have thus assumed the doctrine of predestination as the dogmatic background of the Puritan morality in the sense of methodically rationalized ethical conduct. This could be done because the influence of that dogma in fact extended far beyond the single religious group which held in all respects strictly to Calvinistic principles, the Presbyterians. Not only the Independent Savoy Declaration of 1658, but also the Baptist Confession of Hanserd Knolly of 1689 contained it, and it had a place within Methodism. Although John Wesley, the great organizing genius of the movement, was a believer in the universality of Grace, one of the great agitators of the first generation of Methodists and their most consistent thinker, Whitefield, was an adherent of the doctrine. The same was true of the circle around Lady Huntingdon, which for a time had considerable influence. It was this doctrine in its magnificent consistency which, in the fateful epoch of the seventeenth century, upheld the belief of the militant defenders of the holy life that they were weapons in the hand of God, and executors of His providential Will. Moreover, it prevented a premature collapse into a purely utilitarian doctrine of good works in this world which would never have been capable of motivating such tremendous sacrifices for non-rational ideal ends.

The combination of faith in absolutely valid norms with absolute determinism and the complete transcendentality of God was in its way a product of great genius. At the same time it was, in principle, very much more modern than the milder doctrine, Making greater concessions to the feelings which subjected God to the moral law. Above all, we shall see again and again how fundamental is the idea of proof for our problem. Since its practical significance as a psychological basis for rational morality could be studied in such purity in the doctrine of predestination, it was best to start there with the doctrine in its most consistent form. But it forms a recurring framework. for the connection between faith and conduct in the denominations to be studied below. Within the Protestant movement the consequences which it inevitably had for the ascetic tendencies of the conduct of its first adherents form in principle the strongest antithesis to the relative moral helplessness of Lutheranism. The Lutheran *gratia amissibilis*, which could always be regained through penitent contrition evidently, in itself, contained no sanction for what is for us the most important result of ascetic Protestantism, a systematic rational ordering of the moral life as a whole. The Lutheran faith thus left the spontaneous vitality of impulsive action and naive emotion more nearly unchanged. The motive to constant self-control and thus to a deliberate regulation of one's own life, which the gloomy doctrine of Calvinism gave, was lacking. A religious genius like Luther could live in this atmosphere of openness and freedom without difficulty and, so long as his enthusiasm was powerful enough, without danger of falling back into the *status naturalis*. That simple, sensitive, and peculiarly emotional form of piety, which is the ornament of many of the highest types of Lutherans, like their free and spontaneous morality, finds few parallels in genuine Puritanism, but many more in the mild Anglicanism of such men as Hooker, Chillingsworth, etc. But for the everyday Lutheran, even the able one, nothing was more certain than that he was only temporarily, as long as the single confession or sermon affected' him, raised above the *status naturalis*. There was a great difference which was very striking to contemporaries between the moral standards of the courts of Reformed and of Lutheran princes, the latter often being degraded by drunkenness and vulgarity.

Moreover, the helplessness of the Lutheran clergy, with their emphasis on faith alone, against the ascetic Baptist movement, is well known. The typical German quality often called good nature (*Gemutlichkeit*) or naturalness contrasts strongly, even in the facial expressions of people, with the effects of that thorough destruction of the spontaneity of the *status naturalis* in the Anglo-American atmosphere, which Germans are accustomed to judge unfavourably as narrowness, unfreeness, and inner constraint. But the differences of conduct, which are very striking, have clearly originated in the lesser degree of ascetic penetration of life in Lutheranism as distinguished from Calvinism. The antipathy of every spontaneous child of nature to everything ascetic is expressed in those feelings. The fact is that Lutheranism, on account of its doctrine of grace, lacked a psychological sanction of systematic conduct to compel the methodical rationalization of life.

This sanction, which conditions the ascetic character of religion, could doubtless in itself have been furnished by various different religious motives, as we shall soon see. The Calvinistic doctrine of predestination was only one of several possibilities. But nevertheless we have become convinced that in its way it had not only a quite unique consistency, but that its psychological effect was extraordinarily powerful. In comparison with it the non-Calvinistic ascetic movements, considered purely from the viewpoint of the religious motivation of asceticism, form an attenuation of the inner consistency and power of Calvinism.

But even in the actual historical development the situation was, for the most part, such that the Calvinistic form of asceticism was either imitated by the other ascetic movements or used as a source of inspiration or of comparison in the development of their divergent principles. Where, in spite of a different doctrinal basis, similar ascetic features have appeared, this has generally been the result of Church organization. Of this we shall come to speak in another connection.

B. PIETISM

Historically the doctrine of predestination is also the starting-point of the ascetic movement usually known as Pietism. In so far as the movement remained within the Reformed Church, it is almost impossible to draw the line between Pietistic and non-Pietistic Calvinists. Almost all the leading representatives of Puritanism are sometimes classed among the Pietists. It is even quite legitimate to look upon the whole connection between predestination and the doctrine of proof, with its fundamental interest in the attainment of the *certitudo salutis* as discussed above, as in itself a Pietistic development of Calvin's original doctrines. The occurrence of ascetic revivals within the Reformed Church was, especially in Holland, regularly accompanied by a regeneration of the doctrine of predestination which had been temporarily forgotten or not strictly held to. Hence for England it is not customary to use the term Pietism at all.

But even the Continental (Dutch and Lower Rhenish) Pietism in the Reformed Church was, at least fundamentally, just as much a simple intensification of the Reformed asceticism as, for instance, the doctrines of Bailey. The emphasis was placed so strongly on the *praxis pietatis* that doctrinal orthodoxy was pushed into the background; at times, in fact, it seemed quite a matter of indifference. Those predestined for grace could occasionally be subject to dogmatic error as well as to other sins and experience showed that often those Christians who were quite uninstructed in the theology of the schools exhibited the fruits of faith most clearly, while on the other hand it became evident that mere knowledge of theology by no means guaranteed the proof of faith through conduct.

Thus election could not be proved by theological learning at all. Hence Pietism, with a deep distrust of the

Church of the theologians, to which this is characteristic of it—it still belonged officially, began to gather the adherents of the *praxis pietatis* in conventicles removed from the world. It wished to make the invisible Church of the elect visible on this earth. Without going so far as to form a separate sect, its members attempted to live, in this community, a life freed from all the temptations of the world and in all its details dictated by God's will, and thus to be made certain of their own rebirth by external signs manifested in their daily conduct. Thus the *ecclesiola* of the true converts- this was common to all genuinely Pietistic groups- wished, by means of intensified asceticism, to enjoy the blissfulness of community with God in this life.

Now this latter tendency had something closely, related to the Lutheran *unio mystica*, and very often led to a greater emphasis on the emotional side of religion than was acceptable to orthodox Calvinism. In fact this may, from our view-point, be said to be the decisive characteristic of the Pietism which developed within the Reformed Church. For this element of emotion, which was originally quite foreign to Calvinism, but on the other hand related to certain medieval forms of religion, led religion in practice to strive for the enjoyment of salvation in this world rather than to engage in the ascetic struggle for certainty about the future world. Moreover, the emotion was capable of such intensity, that religion took on a positively hysterical character, resulting in the alternation which is familiar from examples without number and neuro-pathologically understandable, of half-conscious states of religious ecstasy with periods of nervous exhaustion, which were felt as abandonment by God. The effect was the direct opposite of the strict and temperate discipline under which men were placed by the systematic life of holiness of the Puritan. It meant a weakening of the inhibitions which protected the rational personality of the Calvinist from his passions. Similarly it was possible for the Calvinistic idea of the depravity of the flesh, taken emotionally, for instance in the form of the so-called worm-feeling, to lead to a deadening of enterprise in worldly activity. Even the doctrine of predestination could lead to fatalism if, contrary to the predominant tendencies of rational Calvinism, it were made the object of emotional contemplation. Finally, the desire to separate the elect from the world could, with a strong emotional intensity, lead to a sort of monastic community life of half-communistic character, as the history of Pietism, even within the Reformed Church, has shown again and again.

But so long as this extreme effect, conditioned by this emphasis on emotion, did not appear, as long as Reformed Pietism strove to make sure of salvation within the everyday routine of life in a worldly calling, the practical effect of Pietistic principles was an even stricter ascetic control of conduct in the calling, which provided a still more solid religious basis for the ethic of the calling, than the mere worldly respectability of the normal Reformed Christian, which was felt by the superior Pietist to be a second-rate Christianity. The religious aristocracy of the elect, which developed in every form of Calvinistic asceticism, the more seriously it was taken, the more surely, was then organized, in Holland, on a voluntary basis in the form of conventicles within the Church. In English Puritanism, on the other hand, it led partly to a virtual differentiation between active and passive Christians within the Church organization, and partly, as has been shown above, to the formation of sects.

On the other hand, the development of German Pietism from a Lutheran basis, with which the names of Spener, Francke, and Zinzendorf are connected, led away from the doctrine of predestination. But at the same time it was by no means outside the body of ideas of which that dogma formed the logical climax, as is especially attested by Spener's own account of the influence which English and Dutch Pietism had upon him, and is shown by the fact that Bailey was read in his first conventicles.

From our special point of view, at any rate, Pietism meant simply the penetration of methodically controlled and supervised, thus of ascetic, conduct into the non-Calvinistic denominations." But Lutheranism necessarily felt this rational asceticism to be a foreign element, and the lack of consistency in German Pietistic doctrines was the result of the difficulties growing out of that fact. As a dogmatic basis of systematic religious conduct Spener combines Lutheran ideas with the specifically Calvinistic doctrine of good works as such which are undertaken with the "intention of doing honour to God". He also has a faith, suggestive of Calvinism, in the possibility of the elect attaining a relative degree of Christian perfection. But the theory lacked consistency. Spener, who was strongly influenced by the mystics, attempted, in a rather uncertain but essentially Lutheran manner, rather to describe the systematic type of Christian conduct which was essential to even his form of Pietism than to justify it. He did not derive the *certitudo salutis* from sanctification; instead of the idea of proof, he adopted Luther's somewhat loose connection between faith and works, which has been discussed above. But again and again, in so far as the rational and ascetic element of Pietism outweighed the emotional, the ideas essential to our thesis maintained their place.

These were: (1) that the methodical development of one's own state of grace to a higher and higher degree of certainty and perfection in terms of the law was a sign of grace ; and (2) that "God's Providence works through those in such a state of perfection", i.e. in that He gives them His signs if they wait patiently and deliberate methodically. Labour in a calling was also the ascetic activity *par excellence* for A. H. Francke; that God Himself blessed His chosen ones through the success of their labours was as undeniable to him as we shall find it to have been to the Puritans.

And as a substitute for the double decree Pietism worked out ideas which, in a way essentially similar to Calvinism, though milder, established an aristocracy of the elect resting on God's especial grace, with all the psychological results pointed out above. Among them belongs, for instance, the so-called doctrine of Terminism, which was generally (though unjustly) attributed to Pietism by its opponents. It assumes that grace is offered to all men, but for everyone either once at a definite moment in his life or at some moment for the last time. Anyone who let that moment pass was beyond the help of the universality of grace; he was in the same situation as those neglected by God in the Calvinistic doctrine. Quite close to this theory was the idea which Francke took from his personal experience, and which was very widespread in Pietism, one may even say predominant, that grace could only become effective under certain unique and peculiar circumstances, namely, after previous repentance. Since, according to Pietist doctrine, not everyone was capable of such experiences, those who, in spite of the use of the ascetic methods recommended by the Pietists to bring it about, did not attain it, remained in the eyes of the regenerate a sort of passive Christian. On the other hand, by the creation, of a method to induce repentance even the attainment of divine grace became in effect an object of rational human activity.

Moreover, the antagonism to the private confessional, which, though not shared by all-for instance, not by Francke-was characteristic of many Pietists, especially as the repeated questions in Spener show, of Pieti pastors, resulted from this aristocracy of grace. This antagonism helped to weaken its ties with Lutheranism The visible effects on conduct of grace gained through repentance formed a necessary criterion for admission to absolution; hence it was impossible to let *contritio* alone suffice.

Zinzendorf's conception of his own religious position, even though it vacillated in the face of attack from orthodoxy, tended generally toward the instrumental idea. Beyond that, however, the doctrine standpoint of this remarkable religious dilettante, Ritschl calls him, is scarcely capable of clear formulation in the points of importance for us. He repeatedly designated himself a representative of Pauline-Lutheran Christianity; hence he opposed the Pietistic type associated with Jansen with its adherence to the law. But the Brotherhood itself in practice upheld, as early as its Protocol of August 22,

1729, a standpoint which in many respects closely re-
sembled that of the Calvinistic aristocracy of the elect.
And in spite of his repeated avowals of Lutheranism, he
permitted and encouraged it. The famous stand of attrib-
uting the Old Testament to Christ, taken on November 2,
1741, was the outward expression of somewhat the same
attitude. However, of the three branches of the Brotherhood, both the Calvinistic and the Moravian accepted
the Reformed ethics in essentials from the beginning.
And even Zinzendorf followed the Puritans in expressing to John Wesley the opinion that even though a man
himself could not, others could know his state of grace
by his conduct.

But on the other hand, in the peculiar piety of Herrn-
hut, the emotional element held a very prominent place.
In particular Zinzendorf himself continually attempted
to counteract the tendency to ascetic sanctification in
the Puritan sense and to turn the interpretation of good
works in a Lutheran direction. Also under the influence
of the repudiation of conventicles and the retention of
the confession, there developed an essentially Lutheran
dependence on the sacraments. Moreover, Zinzendorf's
peculiar principle that the childlikeness of religious feeling was a sign of its genuineness, as well as the use of
the lot as a means of revealing God's will, strongly counteracted the influence of rationality in conduct. On the
whole, within the sphere of influence of the Count, the
anti-rational, emotional elements predominated much
more in the religion of the Herrnhuters than elsewhere
inpietism. The connection between morality and the
forgiveness of sins in Spangenberg's *Idea fides fratrum* is
as loosel. as in Lutheranism generally. Zinzendorf's repudiation of the Methodist pursuit of perfection is part,
here as everywhere, of his fundamentally eudaemonistic ideal of having men experience eternal bliss (he calls
it happiness) emotionally in the present, instead of en-
couraging them by rational labour to make sure of it in
the next world.

Nevertheless, the idea that the most important value
of the Brotherhood as contrasted with other Churches lay

in an active Christian life, in missionary, and, which was brought into connection with it, in professional work in a calling, remained a vital force with them. In addition, the practical rationalization of life from the standpoint of utility was very essential to Zinzendorf's philosophy. It was derived for him, as for other Pietists, on the one hand from his decided dislike of philosophical speculation as dangerous to faith, and his corresponding preference for empirical knowledge; on the other hand, from the shrewd common sense of the professional missionary. The Brotherhood was, as a great mission centre, at the same time a business enterprise. Thus it led its members into the paths of worldly asceticism, which everywhere first seeks for tasks and then carries them out carefully and systematically. However, the glorification of the apostolic poverty, of the disciples chosen by God through predestination, which was derived from the example of the apostles as missionaries, formed another obstacle. It meant in effect a partial revival of the *consilia evangelica*. The development of a rational economic ethic similar to the Calvinistic was certainly retarded by these factors, even though, as the development of the Baptist movement shows, it was not impossible, but on the contrary subjectively strongly encouraged by the idea of work solely for the sake of the calling.

All in all, when we consider German Pietism from the point of view important for us, we must admit a vacillation and uncertainty in the religious basis of its asceticism which makes it definitely weaker than the iron consistency of Calvinism, and which is partly the result of Lutheran influences and partly of its emotional character. To be sure, it is very one-sided to make this emotional element the distinguishing characteristic of Pietism as opposed to Lutheranism. But compared to Calvinism, the rationalization of life was necessarily less intense because the pressure of occupation with a state of grace which had continually to be proved, and which was concerned for the future in eternity, was diverted to the present emotional state. The place of the self-confidence which the elect sought to attain, and continually to renew in restless and successful work at his calling, was taken by an attitude of humility and abnegation. This in turn was partly the result of emotional stimulus directed solely toward spiritual experience; partly of the Lutheran institution of the confession, which, though it was often looked upon with serious doubts by Pietism, was still generally tolerated. All this shows the influence of the peculiarly Lutheran conception of salvation by the forgiveness of sins and not by practical sanctification. In place of the systematic rational struggle to attain and retain certain knowledge of future (otherworldly) salvation comes here the need to feel reconciliation and community with God now. Thus the tendency of the pursuit of present enjoyment to hinder the rational organization of economic life, depending as it does on provision for the future, has in a certain sense a parallel in the field of religious life.

Evidently, then, the orientation of religious needs to present emotional satisfaction could not develop so powerful a motive to rationalize worldly activity, as the need of the Calvinistic elect for proof with their exclusive preoccupation with the beyond. On the other hand, it was considerably more favourable to the methodical penetration of conduct with religion than the traditionalistic faith of the orthodox Lutheran, bound as it was to the Word and the sacraments. On the whole Pietism from Francke and Spener to Zinzendorf tended toward increasing emphasis on the emotional side. But this was not in any sense the expression of an immanent law of development. The differences resulted from differences of the religious (and social) environments from which the leaders came. We cannot enter into that here, nor can we discuss how the peculiarities of German Pietism have affected its social and geographical extension. We must again remind ourselves that this emotional Pietism of course shades off into the way of life of the Puritan elect by quite gradual stages. If we can, at least provisionally, point out any practical consequence of the difference, we may say that the virtues favoured by Pietism were more those on the one hand of the faithful official, clerk, labourer, or domestic worker, and on the other of the predominantly patriarchal employer with a pious condescension (in Zinzendorf's manner). Calvinism, in comparison, appears to be more closely related to the hard legalism and the active enterprise of bourgeois-capitalistic entrepreneurs. Finally, the purely emotional form of Pietism is, as Ritschl has pointed out, a religious dilettantism for the leisure classes. However far this characterization falls short of being exhaustive, it helps to explain certain differences in the character (including the economic character) of peoples which have been under the influence of one or the other of these two ascetic movements.

C. Methodism

The combination of an emotional but still ascetic type of religion with increasing indifference to or repudiation of the dogmatic basis of Calvinistic asceticism is characteristic also of the Anglo-American movement corresponding to Continental Pietism, namely Methodism. The name in itself shows what impressed contemporaries as characteristic of its adherents: the methodical, systematic nature of conduct for the purpose of attaining the *certitudo salutis*. This was from the beginning the centre of religious aspiration for this movement also, and remained so. In spite of all the differences, the undoubted relationship to certain branches of German Pietism is shown above all by the fact that the method was used primarily to bring about the emotional act of conversion. And the emphasis on feeling, in John Wesley awakened by Moravian and Lutheran influences, led Methodism, which from the beginning saw its mission among the masses, to take on a strongly emotional character, especially in America. The attainment of repentance under certain circumstances involved an emotional struggle of such intensity as to lead to the most terrible ecstasies, which in America often took place in a public meeting. This formed the basis of a belief in the undeserved possession of divine grace and at the same time of an immediate consciousness of justification and forgiveness.

Now this emotional religion entered into a peculiar alliance, containing no small inherent difficulties, with the ascetic ethics which had for good and all been stamped with rationality by Puritanism. For one thing, unlike Calvinism, which held everything emotional to be illusory, the only sure basis for the *certitudo salutis* was in principle held to be a pure feeling of absolute certainty of forgiveness, derived immediately from the testimony of the spirit, the coming of which could be definitely placed to the hour. Added to this is Wesley's doctrine of sanctification which, though a decided departure from the orthodox doctrine, is a logical development of it. According to it, one reborn in this manner can, by virtue of the divine grace already working in him, even in this life attain sanctification, the consciousness of perfection in the sense of freedom from sin, by a second, generally separate and often sudden spiritual transformation. However difficult of attainment this end is, generally not till toward the end of one's life, it must inevitably be sought, because it finally guarantees the *certitudo salutis* and substitutes a serene confidence for the sullen worry of the Calvinist. And it distinguishes the true convert in his own eyes and those of others by the fact that sin at least no longer has power over him.

In spite of the great significance of self-evident feeling, righteous conduct according to the law was thus naturally also adhered to. Whenever Wesley attacked the emphasis on works of his time, it was only to revive the old Puritan doctrine that works are not the cause, but only the means of knowing one's state of grace, and even this only when they are performed solely for the glory of God. Righteous conduct alone did not suffice, as he had found out for himself. The feeling of grace was necessary in addition. He himself sometimes described works as a condition of grace, and in the Declaration of August 9, 1771, he emphasized that he who performed no good works was not a true believer. In fact, the Methodists have always maintained that they did not differ from the Established Church in doctrine, but only in religious practice. This emphasis on the fruits of belief was mostly justified by I John iii, 9; conduct is taken as a clear sign of rebirth.

But in spite of all that there were difficulties. For those Methodists who were adherents of the doctrine of predestination, to think of the *certitudo salutis* as appearing in the immediate feeling of grace and perfection instead of the consciousness of grace which grew out of ascetic conduct in continual proof of faith since then the certainty of the *perservantia* depended only on the single act of repentance-meant one of two things. For weak natures there was a fatalistic interpretation of Christian freedom, and with it the breakdown of methodical conduct; or, where this path was rejected, the self-confidence of the righteous man reached untold heights, an emotional intensification of the Puritan type. In the face of the attacks of opponents, the attempt was made to meet these consequences. On the one hand by increased emphasis on the normative authority of the Bible and the indispensability of proof ; on the other by, in effect, strengthening Wesley's anti-Calvinistic faction within the movement with its doctrine that grace could be lost. The strong Lutheran influences to which Wesley was exposed through the Moravians strengthened this tendency and increased the uncertainty of the religious basis of the Methodist ethics. In the end only the concept of regeneration, an emotional certainty of salvation as the immediate result of faith, was definitely maintained as the indispensable foundation of grace; and with it sanctification, resulting in (at least virtual) freedom from the power of sin, as the consequent proof of grace. The significance of external means of grace, especially the sacraments, was correspondingly diminished. In any case, the general awakening which followed Methodism everywhere, for example in New England, meant a victory for the doctrine of grace and election .

Thus from our view-point the Methodist ethic appears to rest on a foundation of uncertainty similar to Pietism. But the aspiration to the higher life, the second blessedness, served it as a sort of makeshift for the doctrine of predestination. Moreover, being English in origin, its ethical practice was closely related to that of English Puritanism, the revival of which it aspired to be. The emotional act of conversion was methodically induced. And after it was attained there did not follow a pious enjoyment of community with God, after the manner of the emotional Pietism of Zinzendorf, but the emotion, once awakened, was directed into a rational struggle for perfection. Hence the emotional character of its faith did not lead to a spiritualized religion of feeling like German Pietism. It has already been shown by Schneckenburger that this fact was connected with the less intensive. development of the sense of sin (partly directly on account of the emotional experience of conversion), and this has remained an accepted point in the discussion of Methodism. The fundamentally Calvinistic character of its religious feeling here remained decisive. The emotional excitement took the form of enthusiasm which was only occasionally, but then powerfully stirred, but which by no means destroyed the otherwise rational character of conduct. The regeneration of Methodism thus created only a supplement to the pure doctrine of works, a religious basis for ascetic conduct after the doctrine of predestination had been given up. The signs given by conduct which formed an indispensable means of ascertaining true conversion, even its condition as Wesley occasionally says, were in fact just the same as those of Calvinism. As a late product we can, in the following discussion, generally neglect Methodism, as it added nothing new to the development of the idea of calling.

D. THE BAPTIST SECTS

The Pietism of the Continent of Europe and the Methodism of the Anglo-Saxon peoples are, considered both in their content of ideas and their historical significance, secondary movements. On the other hand, we find a second independent source of Protestant asceticism besides Calvinism in the Baptist movement and the sects which, in the course of the sixteenth and seventeenth centuries, came directly from it or adopted its forms of religious thought, the Baptists, Mennonites, and, above all, the Quakers. With them we approach religious groups whose ethics rest upon a basis differing in principle from the Calvinistic doctrine. The following sketch, which only emphasizes what is important for us, can give no true impression of the diversity of this movement. Again we lay the principal emphasis on the development in the older capitalistic countries.

The feature of all these communities, which is both historically and in principle most important, but whose influence on the development of culture can only be made quite clear in a somewhat different connection, is something with which we are already familiar, the believer's Church .This means that the religious community, the visible Church in the language of the Reformation Churches, was no longer looked upon as a sort of trust foundation for supernatural ends, an institution, necessarily including both the just and the unjust, whether for increasing the glory of God (Calvinistic) or as a medium for bringing the means of salvation to men (Catholic and Lutheran), but solely as a community of personal believers of the reborn, and only these. In other words, not as a Church but as a Sect. This is all that the principle, in itself purely external, that only adults who have personally gained their own faith should be baptized, is meant to symbolize. The justification through this faith was for the Baptists, as they have insistently repeated in all religious discussions, radically different from the idea of work in the world in the service of Christ, such as dominated the orthodox dogma of the older Protestantism. It consisted rather in taking spiritual possession of His gift of salvation. But this occurred through individual revelation, by the working of the Divine Spirit in the individual, and only in that way. It was offered to everyone, and it sufficed to wait for the Spirit, and not to resist its coming by a sinful attachment to the world. The significance of faith in the sense of knowledge of the doctrines of the Church, but also in that of a repentant search for divine grace, was consequently quite minimized, and there took place, naturally with great modifications, a renaissance of Early Christian pneumatic doctrines. For instance, the sect to which Menno Simons in his *Fondamentboek* (1539) gave the first reasonably consistent doctrine, wished, like the other Baptist sects, to be the true blameless Church of Christ; like the apostolic community, consisting entirely of those personally awakened and called by God. Those who have been born again, and they alone, are brethren of Christ, because they, like Him, have been created in spirit directly by God. A strict avoidance of the world, in the sense of all not strictly necessary intercourse with worldly people, together with the strictest bibliocracy in the sense of taking the life of the first generations of Christians as a model, were the results for the first Baptist communities, and this principle of avoidance of the world never quite disappeared so long as the old spirit remained alive.

As a permanent possession, the Baptist sects retained from these dominating motives of their early period a principle with which, on a somewhat different foundation, we have already become acquainted in Calvinism, and the fundamental importance of which will again and again come out. They absolutely repudiated all idolatry of the flesh, as a detraction from the reverence due to God alone The Biblical way of life was conceived by the first Swiss and South German Baptists with a radicalism similar to that of the young St. Francis, as a sharp break with all the enjoyment of life, a life modelled directly on that of the Apostles. And, in truth, the life of many of the earlier Baptists is reminiscent of that of St. Giles. But this strict observation of Biblical precepts was not on very secure foundations in its connection with the pneumatic character of the faith. What God had revealed to the prophets and apostles was not all that He could and would reveal. On the contrary, the continued life of the Word, not as a written document, but as the force of the Holy Spirit working in daily life, which speaks directly to any individual who is willing to hear, was the sole characteristic of the true Church. That, as Schwenkfeld taught as against Luther and later Fox against the Presbyterians, was the testimony of the early Christian communities. From this idea of the continuance of revelation developed the well-known doctrine, later consistently worked out by the Quakers, of the (in the last analysis decisive) significance of the inner testimony of the Spirit in reason and conscience. This did away, not with the authority, but with the sole authority, of the Bible, and started a development which in the end radically eliminated all that remained of the doctrine of salvation through the Church; for the Quakers even with Baptism and the Communion.

The Baptist denominations along with the predestinationists, especially the strict Calvinists, carried out the most radical devaluation of all sacraments as means to salvation, and thus accomplished the religious rationalization of the world in its most extreme form. Only the inner light of continual revelation could enable one truly to understand even the Biblical revelations of God. On the other hand, at least according to the Quaker doctrine which here drew the logical conclusion, its effects could be extended to people who had never known revelation in its Biblical form. The proposition *extra ecclesiam nulla salus* held only for this *in*visible Church of those illuminated by the Spirit. Without the inner light, the natural man, even the man guided by natural reason, remained purely a creature of the flesh, whose godlessness was condemned by the Baptists, including the Quakers, almost even more harshly than by the Calvinists. On the other hand, the new birth caused by the Spirit, if we wait for it and open our hearts to it, may, since it is divinely caused, lead to a state of such complete conquest of the power of sin that relapses, to say nothing of the loss of the state of grace, become practically impossible. However, as in Methodism at a later time, the attainment of that state was not thought of as the rule, but rather the degree of perfection of the individual was subject to development.

But all Baptist communities desired to be pure Churches in the sense of the blameless conduct of their members. A sincere repudiation of the world and its interests, and unconditional submission to God as speaking through the conscience, were the only unchallengeable signs of true rebirth, and a corresponding type of conduct was thus indispensable to salvation. And hence the gift of God's grace could not be earned, but only one who followed the dictates of his conscience could be justified in considering himself reborn. Good works in this sense were a *causa sine qua non*. As we see, this last reasoning of Barclay, to whose exposition we have adhered, was again the equivalent in practice of the Calvinistic doctrine, and was certainly developed under the influence of the Calvinistic asceticism, which surrounded the Baptist sects in England and the Netherlands. George Fox devoted the whole of his early missionary activity to the preaching of its earnest and sincere adoption.

But, since predestination was rejected, the peculiarly rational character of Baptist morality rested psychologically above all on the idea of expectant waiting for the Spirit to descend, which even today is characteristic of the Quaker meeting, and is well analysed by Barclay. The purpose of this silent waiting is to overcome everything impulsive and irrational, the passions and subjective interests of the natural man. He must be stilled in order to create that deep repose of the soul in which alone the word of God can be heard. Of course, this waiting might result in hysterical conditions, prophecy, and, as long as eschatological hopes survived, under certain circumstances even in an outbreak of chiliastic enthusiasm, as is possible in all similar types of religion. That actually happened in the movement which went to pieces in Munster.

But in so far as Baptism affected the normal workaday world, the idea that God only speaks when the flesh is silent evidently meant an incentive to the deliberate weighing of courses of action and their careful justification in terms of the individual conscience. The later Baptist communities, most particularly the Quakers, adopted this quiet, moderate, eminently conscientious character of conduct. The radical elimination of magic from the world allowed no other psychological course than the practice of worldly asceticism. Since these communities would have nothing to do with the political powers and their doings, the external result also was the penetration of life in the calling with these ascetic virtues. The leaders of the earliest Baptist movement were ruthlessly radical in their rejection of worldliness. But naturally,even in the first generation, the strictly apostolic way of life was not maintained as absolutely essential to the proof of rebirth for everyone. Well-to-do bourgeois there were, even in this generation and even before Menno, who definitely defended the practical worldly virtues and the system of private property; the strict morality of the Baptists had turned in practice into the path prepared by the Calvinistic ethic. This was simply because the road to the otherworldly monastic form of asceticism had been closed as unbiblical and savouring of salvation by works since Luther, whom the Baptists also followed in this respect.

Nevertheless, apart from the half-communistic communities of the early period, one Baptist sect, the so-called Dunckards (*Tunker, dompelaers*), has to this day maintained its condemnation of education and of every form of possession beyond that indispensable to life. And even Barclay looks upon the obligation to one's calling not in Calvinistic or even Lutheran terms, but rather Thomistically, as *naturali ratione*, the necessary consequence of the believers, having to live in the world.

This attitude meant a weakening of the Calvinistic conception of the calling similar to those of Spener and the German Pietists. But, on the other hand, the intensity of interest in economic occupations was considerably increased by various factors at work in the Baptist sects. In the first place, by the refusal to accept office in the service of the State, which originated as a religious duty following from the repudiation of everything worldly. After its abandonment in principle it still remained, at least for the Mennonites and Quakers, effective in practice, because the strict refusal to bear arms or to take oaths formed a sufficient disqualification for office. Hand in hand with it in all Baptists' denominations went an invincible antagonism to any sort of aristocratic way of life. Partly, as with the Calvinists, it was a consequence of the prohibition of all idolatry of the flesh, partly a result of the aforementioned unpolitical or even anti-political principles, The whole shrewd and conscientious rationality of Baptist conduct was thus forced into non-political callings.

At the same time, the immense importance which was attributed by the Baptist doctrine of salvation to the role of the conscience as the revelation of God to the individual gave their conduct in worldly callings a character which was of the greatest significance for the development of the spirit of capitalism. We shall have to postpone its consideration until later, and it can then be studied only in so far as this is possible without entering into the whole political and social ethics of Protestant asceticism. But, to anticipate this much, we have already called attention to that most important principle of the capitalistic ethic which is generally formulated "honesty is the best policy" Its classical document is the tract of Franklin quoted above. And even in the judgment of the seventeenth century the specific form of the worldly asceticism of the Baptists, especially the Quakers, lay in the practical adoption of this maxim.1m On the other hand, we shall expect to find that the influence of Calvinism was exerted more in the direction of the liberation of energy for private acquisition. For in spite of all the formal legalism of the elect, Goethe's remark in fact applied often enough to the Calvinist: "The man of action is always ruthless; no one has a conscience but an observer."

A further important element which promoted the intensity of the worldly asceticism of the Baptist denominations can in its full significance also be considered only in another connection. Nevertheless, we may anticipate a few remarks on it to justify the order of presentation we have chosen. We have quite deliberately not taken as a starting point the objective social institutions of the older Protestant Churches, and their ethical influences, especially not the very important Church discipline. We have preferred rather to take the results which subjective adoption of an ascetic faith might have had in the conduct of the individual. This was not only because this side of the thing has previously received far less attention than the other, but also because the effect of Church discipline was by no means always a similar one. On the contrary, the ecclesiastical supervision of the life of the individual, which, as it was practised in the Calvinistic State Churches, almost amounted to an inquisition, might even retard that liberation of individual powers which was conditioned by the rational ascetic pursuit of salvation, and in some cases actually did so.

The mercantilistic regulations of the State might develop industries, but not, or certainly not alone, the spirit of capitalism; where they assumed a despotic, authoritarian character, they to a large extent directly hindered it. Thus a similar effect might well have resulted from ecclesiastical regimentation when it became excessively despotic. It enforced a particular type of external conformity, but in some cases weakened the subjective motives of rational conduct. Any discussion of this point must take account of the great difference between the results of the authoritarian moral discipline of the Established Churches and tile corresponding discipline in the sects which rested on voluntary submission. That the Baptist movement everywhere and in principle founded sects and not Churches was certainly as favourable to the intensity of their asceticism as was the case, to differing degrees, with those Calvinistic, Methodist, and Pietist communities which were driven by their situations into the formation of voluntary groups.

It is our next task to follow out the results of the Puritan idea of the calling in the business world, now that the above sketch has attempted to show its religious foundations. With all the differences of detail and emphasis which these different ascetic movements show in the aspects with which we have been concerned, much the same characteristics are present and important in all of them. But for our purposes the decisive point was, to recapitulate, the conception of the state of religious grace, common to all the denominations, as a status which marks off its possessor from the degradation of the flesh, from the world.

On the other hand, though the means by which it was attained differed for different doctrines, it could not be guaranteed by any magical sacraments, by relief in the confession, nor by individual good works. That was only possible by proof in a specific type of conduct unmistakably different from the way of life of the natural man. From that followed for the individual an incentive methodically to supervise his own state of grace in his own conduct, and thus to penetrate it with asceticism. But, as we have seen, this ascetic conduct meant a rational planning of the whole of one's life in accordance with God's will. And this asceticism was no longer an *opus supererogationis*, but something which could be required of everyone who would be certain of salvation. The religious life of the saints, as distinguished from the natural life, was the most important point-no longer lived outside the world in monastic communities, but within the world and its institutions. This rationalization of conduct within this world, but for the sake of the world beyond, was the consequence of the concept of calling of ascetic J Protestantism.

Christian asceticism, at first fleeing from the world into solitude, had already ruled the world which it had renounced from the monastery and through the Church. But it had, on the whole, left the naturally spontaneous character of daily life in the world untouched. Now it strode into the marketplace of life slammed the door of the monastery behind it, an undertook to penetrate just that daily routine of life with its methodicalness, to fashion it into a life in the world, but neither of nor for this world. With what result, we shall try to make clear in the following discussion.

Chapter V.

ASCETICISM AND THE SPIRIT OF CAPITALISM

In order to understand the connection between the fundamental religious ideas of ascetic Protestantism and its maxims for everyday economic conduct, it is necessary to examine with especial care such writings as have evidently been derived from ministerial practice. For in a time in which the beyond meant everything, when the social position of the Christian depended upon his admission to the communion, the clergyman, through his ministry, Church discipline, and preaching, exercised an influence (as a glance at collections of *consilia, casus conscientiae*, etc., shows) which we modern men are entirely unable to picture. In such a time the religious forces which express themselves through such channels are the decisive influences in the formation of national character.

For the purposes of this chapter, though by no means for all purposes, we can treat ascetic Protestantism as a single whole. But since that side of English Puritanism which was derived from Calvinism gives the most consistent religious basis for the idea of the calling, we shall, following our previous method, place one of its representatives at the centre of the discussion. Richard Baxter stands out above many other writers on Puritan ethics, both because of his eminently practical and realistic attitude, and, at the same time, because of the universal recognition accorded to his works, which have gone through many new editions and translations. He was a Presbyterian and an apologist of the Westminster Synod, but at the same time, like so many of the best spirits of his time, gradually grew away from the dogmas of pure Calvinism. At heart he opposed Cromwell's usurpation as he would any revolution. He was unfavourable to the sects and the fanatical enthusiasm of the saints, but was very broadminded about external peculiarities and objective towards his opponents. He sought his field of labour most especially in the practical promotion of the moral life through the Church. In the pursuit of this end, as one of the most successful ministers known to history, he placed his services at the disposal of the Parliamentary Government, of Cromwell, and of the Restoration,' until he retired, from office under the last, before St. Bartholomew's day. His *Christian Directory* is the most compendium of Puritan ethics, and is c adjusted to the practical experiences of his of his own ministerial activity. In comparison we shall make use of Spener's *Theologische Bedenken*, as representative o German Pietism, Barclay's *Apology* for the Quakers and some other representatives of ascetic ethics, which, however, in the interest of space, will be limited as far as possible.

Now, in glancing at Baxter's Saints' *Everlasting Rest*, or his *Christian Directory*, or similar works of others, one is struck at first glance by the emphasis placed, in the discussion of wealth and its acquisition, on the ebionitic elements of the New testament. Wealth as such is a great danger; its temptations never end and its pursuit is not only senseless as compared with the dominating importance of the Kingdom of God, but it-is morally suspect. Here asceticism seems to have turned much more sharply against the acquisition of earthly goods than it did in Calvin, who saw no hindrance to the effectiveness of the clergy in their wealth, but rather a thoroughly desirable enhancement of their prestige. Hence he permitted them to employ their means profitably. Examples of the condemnation of the pursuit of money and goods may be gathered without end from Puritan writings, and may be contrasted with the late medieval ethical literature, which was much more open-minded on this point. Moreover, these doubts were meant with perfect seriousness; only it is necessary to examine them somewhat more closely in order to understand their true ethical significance and implications. The real. moral objection is to relaxation in the security of possession, the enjoyment of wealth with the consequence of idleness and the temptations of the flesh, above all of distraction from the pursuit of a righteous life. In fact, it is only because possession involves this danger of relaxation that it is objectionable at all. For the saints' everlasting rest is in the next world; on earth man must, to be certain of his state of grace, "do the works of him who sent him, as long as it is yet day". Not leisure and enjoyment, but only activity serves to increase the glory of God, according to the definite manifestations of His will.

Waste of time is thus the first and in principle the deadliest of sins. The span of human life is infinitely short and precious to make sure of one's own election. Loss of time through sociability, idle talk, luxury," even more sleep than is necessary for health, six to at most eight hours, is worthy of absolute moral condemnation. It does not yet hold, with Franklin, that time is money, but the proposition is true in a certain spiritual sense. It is infinitely valuable because every hour lost is lost to labour for the glory of God. Thus inactive contemplation is also valueless, or even directly reprehensible if it is at the expense of one's daily work. For it is less pleasing to God than the active performance of His will in a calling. Besides, Sunday is provided for that, and, according to Baxter, it is always those who are not diligent in their callings who have no time for God when the occasion demands it.

Accordingly, Baxter's principal work is dominated by the continually repeated, often almost passionate preaching of hard, continuous bodily or mental labour. It is due to a combination of two different motives. Labour is, on the one hand, an approved ascetic technique, as it always has been in the Western Church, in sharp contrast not only to the Orient but to almost all monastic rules the world over. It is in particular the specific defence against all those temptations which Puritanism united under the name of the unclean life, whose role for it was by no means small. The sexual asceticism of Puritanism differs only in degree, not in fundamental principle, from that of monasticism; and on account of the Puritan conception of marriage, its practical influence is more far reaching than that of the latter. For sexual intercourse is permitted, even within marriage, only as the means willed by God for the increase of His glory according to the commandment, "Be fruitful and Multiply." Along with a moderate vegetable diet and cold baths, the same prescription is given for all sexual temptations as is used against religious doubts and a sense of moral unworthiness: "Work hard in your calling." But the most important thing was that even beyond that labour came to he considered in itself the end of life, ordained as such by God. St. Paul's "He who will not work shall not eat" holds unconditionally for every-one. Unwillingness to work is symptomatic of the lack of grace.

Here the difference from the medieval view-point becomes quite evident. Thomas Aquinas also gave an interpretation of that statement of St. Paul. But for him labour is only necessary *naturali ratione* for the maintenance of individual and community. Where this end is achieved, the precept ceases to have any meaning. Moreover, it holds only for the race, not for every individual. It does not apply to anyone who can live without labour on his possessions, and of course contemplation, as a spiritual form of action in the Kingdom of God, takes precedence over the commandment in its literal sense. Moreover, for the popular theology of the time, the highest form of monastic productivity lay in the increase of the *Thesaurus ecclesiae* through prayer and chant.

Now only do these exceptions to the duty to labour naturally no longer hold for Baxter, but he holds most emphatically that wealth does not exempt anyone from the unconditional command. Even the wealthy shall not cat without working, for even though they do not need to labour to support their own needs, there is God's commandment which they, like the poor, must obey. For everyone without exception God's Providence has prepared a calling, which he should profess and in which he should labour. And this calling is not, as it was for the Lutheran, a fate to which he must submit and which he must make the best of, but God's commandment to the individual to work for the divine glory. This seemingly subtle difference had far-reaching psychological consequences, and became connected with a further development of the providential interpretation of the economic order which had begun in scholasticism.

The phenomenon of the division of labour and occupations in society had, among others, been interpreted by Thomas Aquinas, to whom we may most conveniently refer, as a direct consequence of the divine scheme of things. But the places assigned to each man in this cosmos follow *ex causis naturalibus* and are fortuitous (contingent in the Scholastic terminology). The differentiation of men into the classes and occupations established through historical development became for Luther, as we have seen, a direct result of the divine will. The perseverance of the individual in the place and within the limits which God had assigned to him was a religious duty. This was the more certainly the consequence since the relations of Lutheranism to the world were in general uncertain from the beginning and remained so. Ethical principles for the reform of the world could not be found in Luther's realm of ideas; in fact it never quite freed itself from Pauline indifference. Hence the world had to be accepted as it was, and this alone could be made a religious duty.

But in the Puritan view, the providential character of the play of private economic interests takes on a somewhat different emphasis. True to the Puritan tendency to pragmatic interpretations, the providential purpose of the division of labour is to be known by its fruits. On this point Baxter expresses himself in terms which more than once directly recall Adam Smith's well-known apotheosis of the division of labour. The specialization of occupations leads, since it makes the development of skill possible, to a quantitative and qualitative improvement in production, and thus serves the common good, which is identical with the good of the greatest possible number. So far, the motivation is purely utilitarian, and is closely related to the customary view-point of much of the secular literature of the time.

But the characteristic Puritan element appears when Baxter sets at the head of his discussion the statement that "outside of a well-marked calling the accomplishments of a man are only casual and irregular, and he spends more time in idleness than at work", and when he concludes it as follows: "and he [the specialized worker] will carry out his work in order while another remains in constant confusion, and his business knows neither time nor place...therefore is a certain calling the best for everyone". Irregular work, which the ordinary labourer is often forced to accept, is often unavoidable, but always an unwelcome state of transition. A man without a calling thus lacks the systematic, methodical character which is, as we have seen, demanded by worldly asceticism.

The Quaker ethic also holds that a man's life in his calling is an exercise in ascetic virtue, a proof of his state of grace through his conscientiousness, which is expressed in the care and method with which he pursues his calling. What God demands is not labour in itself, but rational labour in a calling. In the Puritan concept of the calling the emphasis is always placed on this methodical character of worldly asceticism, not, as with Luther, on the acceptance of the lot which God has irretrievably assigned to man.

Hence the question whether anyone may combine several callings is answered in the affirmative, if it is useful for the common good or one's own, and not injurious to anyone, and if it does not lead to unfaithfulness in one of the callings. Even a change of calling is by no means regarded as objectionable, if it is not thoughtless and is made for the purpose of pursuing a calling more pleasing to God,which means, on general principles, one more useful.

It is true that the usefulness of a calling, and thus its favour in the sight of God, is measured primarily in moral terms, and thus in terms of the importance of the goods produced in it for the community. But a further, and, above all, in practice the most important, criterion is found in private profitableness. For if that God, whose hand the Puritan sees in all the occurrences of life, shows one of His elect a chance of profit, he must do it with a purpose. Hence the faithful Christian must follow the call by taking advantage of the opportunity. "If God show you a way in which you may lawfully get more than in another way (without wrong to your soul or to any other), if you refuse this, and choose the less gainful way, you cross one of the ends of your calling, and you refuse to be God's steward, and to accept His gifts and use them for Him, when He requireth it: you may labour to be rich for God, though not for the flesh and sin."

Wealth is thus bad ethically only in so far as it is a temptation to idleness and sinful enjoyment of life, and its acquisition is bad only when it is with the purpose of later living merrily and without care. But as a performance of duty in a calling it is not only morally permissible, but actually enjoined .The parable of the servant who was rejected because he did not increase the talent which was entrusted to him seemed to say so directly. To wish to be poor was, it was often argued, the same as wishing to be unhealthy ; it is objectionable as a glorification of works and derogatory to the glory of God. Especially begging, on the part of one able to work, is not only the sin of slothfulness, but a violation of the duty of brotherly love according to the Apostle's own word.

The emphasis on the ascetic importance of a fixed calling provided an ethical justification of the modern specialized division of labour. In a similar way the providential interpretation of profit-making justified the activities of the business man. The superior indulgence of the *seigneur* and the parvenu ostentation of the *nouveau riche* are equally detestable to asceticism. But, on the other hand, it has the highest ethical appreciation of the sober, middle-class, self-made Man. "God blesseth His trade" is a stock remark about those good men who had successfully followed the divine hints. The whole power of the God of the Old Testament, who rewards His people for their obedience in this life, necessarily exercised a similar influence on the Puritan who, following Baxter's advice, compared his own state of grace with that of the heroes of the Bible, and in the process interpreted the statements of the Scriptures as the articles of a book of statutes.

Of course, the words of the Old Testament were not entirely without ambiguity. We have seen that Luther first used the concept of the calling in the secular sense in translating a passage from Jesus Sirach. But the book of Jesus Sirach belongs, with the whole atmosphere expressed in it, to those parts of the broadened Old Testament with distinctly traditionalistic tendency, in spite of Hellenistic influences. It is characteristic that down to the present day this book seems to enjoy a special favour among Lutheran German peasants just as the Lutheran influence in large sections of German Pietism has been expressed by a preference for Jesus Sirach.

The Puritans repudiated the Apocrypha as not inspired, consistently with their sharp distinction between things divine and things of the flesh. But among the canonical books that of Job had all the more influence. On the one hand it contained a grand conception of the absolute sovereign majesty, of God, beyond all human comprehension, which was closely related to that of Calvinism. With that, on the other hand, it combined the certainty which, though incidental for Calvin, came to be of great importance for Puritanism, that God would bless His own in this life -in the book of Job only-and also in the material sense .The Oriental quietism, which appears in several of the finest verses of the Psalms and in the Proverbs, was interpreted away, just as Baxter did with the traditionalistic tinge of the passage in the 1st Epistle to the Corinthians, so important for the idea of the calling.

But all the more emphasis was placed on those parts of the Old Testament which praise formal legality as a sign of conduct pleasing to God. They held the theory that the Mosaic Law had only lost its validity through

Christ in so far as it contained ceremonial or purely historical precepts applying only to the Jewish people, but that otherwise it had always been valid as an expression of the natural law, and must hence be retained. This made it possible, on the one hand, to eliminate elements which could not be reconciled with modern life. But still, through its numerous related features, Old Testament morality was able to give a powerful impetus to that spirit of self-righteous and sober legality which was so characteristic of the worldly asceticism of this form of Protestantism."

Thus when authors, as was the case with several contemporaries as well as later writers, characterize the basic ethical tendency of Puritanism, especially in England, as English Hebrews they are, correctly understood, not wrong. It is necessary, however, not to think of Palestinian Judaism at the time of the writing of the Scriptures, but of Judaism as it became under the influence of many centuries of formalistic, legalistic, and Talmudic education. Even then one must be very careful in drawing parallels. The general tendency of the older Judaism toward a naive acceptance of life as such was far removed from the special characteristics of Puritanism. It was, however, just as far-and this ought not to be overlooked-from the economic ethics of medieval and modern Judaism, in the traits which determined the positions of both in the development of the capitalistic ethos. The Jews stood on the side of the politically and speculatively oriented adventurous capitalism; their ethos was, in a word, that of pariah-capitalism. But Puritanism carried the ethos of the rational organization of capital and labour. It took over from the Jewish ethic only what was adapted to this purpose.

To analyse the effects on the character of peoples of the penetration of life with Old Testament norms—a tempting task which, however, has not yet satisfactorily been done even for Judaism—would be impossible within the limits of this sketch. In addition to the relationships already pointed out, it is important for the general inner attitude of the Puritans, above all, that the belief that they were God's chosen people saw in them a great renaissance. Even the kindly Baxter thanked God that he was born in England, and thus in the true Church, and nowhere else. This thankfulness for one's own perfection by the grace of God penetrated the attitude toward life of the Puritan middle class, and played its part in developing that formalistic, hard, correct character which was peculiar to the men of that heroic age of capitalism.

Let us now try to clarify the points in which the Puritan idea of the calling and the premium it placed upon ascetic conduct was bound directly to influence the development of a capitalistic way of life. As we have seen, this asceticism turned with all its force against one thing: the spontaneous enjoyment of life and all it had to offer. This is perhaps most characteristically brought out in the struggle over the *Book of Sports* which James I and Charles I made into law expressly as a means of counteracting Puritanism, and which the latter ordered to be read from all the pulpits. The fanatical opposition of the Puritans to the ordinances of the King, permitting certain popular amusements on Sunday outside of Church hours by law, was not only explained by the disturbance of the Sabbath rest, but also by resentment against the intentional diversion from the ordered life of the saint, which it caused. And, on his side, the King's threats of severe punishment for every attack on the legality of those sports were motivated by his purpose of breaking the anti-authoritarian ascetic tendency of Puritanism, which was so dangerous to the State. The feudal and monarchical forces protected the pleasure seekers against the rising middle-class morality and the anti-authoritarian ascetic conventicles, just as today capitalistic society tends to protect those willing to work against the class morality of the proletariat and the anti-authoritarian trade union.

As against this the Puritans upheld their decisive characteristic, the principle of ascetic conduct. For otherwise the Puritan aversion to sport, even for the Quakers, was by no means simply one of principle. Sport was accepted if it served a rational purpose, that of recreation necessary for physical efficiency. But as a means for the spontaneous expression of undisciplined impulses, it was under suspicion; and in so far as it became purely a means of enjoyment, or awakened pride, raw instincts or the irrational gambling instinct, it was of course strictly condemned. Impulsive enjoyment of life, which leads away both from work in a calling and from religion, was as such the enemy of rational asceticism, whether in the form of seigneurial sports, or the enjoyment of the dance-hall or the public-house of the common man.

Its attitude was thus suspicious and often hostile to the aspects of culture without any immediate religious value. It is not, however, true that the ideals of Puritanism implied a solemn, narrow-minded contempt of culture. Quite the contrary is the case at least for science, with the exception of the hatred of Scholasticism. Moreover, the great men of the Puritan movement were thoroughly steeped in the culture of the Renaissance. The sermons of the Presbyterian divines abound with classical allusions and even the Radicals, although they objected to it, were not ashamed to display that kind of learning in theological polemics. Perhaps no country, was ever so full of graduates as New England in the first generation of its existence. The satire of their opponents, such as, for instance, Butler's *Hudibras*, also attacks primarily the pedantry and highly trained dialectics of the Puritans. This is partially due to the religious valuation of knowledge which followed from their attitude to the Catholic *fides implicita*.

But the situation is quite different when one looks at non-scientific literature and especially the fine arts. Here asceticism descended like a frost on the life of "Merrie old England." And not only worldly merriment felt its effect. The Puritan's ferocious hatred of everything which smacked of superstition, of all survivals of magical or sacramental salvation, applied to the Christmas festivities and the May Pole and all spontaneous religious art. That there was room in Holland for a great, often uncouthly realistic art proves only how far from completely the authoritarian moral discipline of that country was able to counteract the influence of the court and the regents (a class of *rentiers*), and also the joy in life of the parvenu bourgeoisie, after the short supremacy of the Calvinistic theocracy had been transformed into a moderate national Church, and with it Calvinism had perceptibly lost in its power of ascetic influence.

The theatre was obnoxious to the Puritans, and with the strict exclusion of the erotic and of nudity from the realm of toleration, a radical view of either literature or art could not exist. The conceptions of idle talk, of superfluities, and of vain ostentation, all designations of an irrational attitude without objective purpose, thus not ascetic, and especially not serving the glory of God, but of man, were always at hand to serve in deciding in favour of sober utility as against any artistic tendencies. This was especially true in the case of decoration of the person, for instance clothing. That powerful tendency toward uniformity of life, which today so immensely aids the capitalistic interest in the standardization of production," had its ideal foundations in the repudiation of all idolatry of the flesh.

Of course we must not forget that Puritanism included a world of contradictions, and that the instinctive sense of eternal greatness in art was certainly stronger among its leaders than in the atmosphere of the Cavaliers. Moreover, a unique genius like Rembrandt, however little his conduct may have been acceptable to God in the eyes of the Puritans, was very strongly influenced in the character of his work by his religious environment. But that does not alter the picture as a whole. In so far as the development of the Puritan tradition could, and in part did, lead to a powerful spiritualization of personality, it was a decided benefit to literature. But for the most part that benefit only accrued to later generations.

Although we cannot here enter upon a discussion of the influence of Puritanism in all these directions, we should call attention to the fact that the toleration of pleasure in cultural goods, which contributed to purely aesthetic or athletic enjoyment, certainly always ran up against one characteristic limitation: they must not cost anything. Man is only a trustee of the goods which "have come to him through God's grace. He must, like the servant in the parable, give an account of every penny entrusted to him, and it is at least hazardous to spend any of it for a purpose which does not serve the glory of God but only one's own enjoyment. What person, who keeps his eyes open, has not met representatives of this view-point even in the present? The idea of a man's duty to his possessions, to which he subordinates himself as an obedient steward, or even as an acquisitive machine, bears with chilling weight on his life. The greater the possessions the heavier, if the ascetic attitude toward life stands the test, the feeling of responsibility for them, for holding them undiminished for the glory of God and increasing them by restless effort. The origin of this type of life also extends in certain roots, like so many aspects of the spirit of capitalism, back into the Middle Ages. But it was in the ethic of ascetic Protestantism that it first r found a consistent ethical foundation. Its significance for the development of capitalism is obvious.

This worldly Protestant asceticism, as we may recapitulate up to this point, acted powerfully against the spontaneous enjoyment of possessions; it restricted consumption, especially of luxuries. On the other hand, it had the psychological effect of freeing the acquisition of goods from the inhibitions of traditionalistic ethics. It broke the bonds of the impulse of acquisition in that it not only legalized it, but (in the sense discussed) looked upon it as directly willed by God. The campaign against the temptations of the flesh, and the dependence on external things, was, as besides the Puritans the great Quaker apologist Barclay expressly says, not a struggle against the rational acquisition, but against the irrational use of wealth.

But this irrational use was exemplified in the outward forms of luxury which their code condemned as idolatry of the flesh, however natural they had appeared to the feudal mind. On the other hand, they approved the rational and utilitarian uses of wealth which were willed by God for the needs of the individual and the community. They did not wish to impose mortification on the man of wealth, but the use of his means for necessary and practical things. The idea of comfort characteristically limits the extent of ethically permissible expenditures. It is naturally no accident that the development of a manner of living consistent with that idea may be observed earliest and most clearly among the most consistent representatives of this whole attitude toward life. Over against the glitter and ostentation of feudal magnificence which, resting on an unsound economic basis, prefers a sordid elegance to a sober simplicity, they set the clean and solid comfort of the middle-class home as an ideal."

On the side of the production of private wealth, asceticism condemned both dishonesty and impulsive avarice. What was condemned as covetousness, Mammonism, etc., was the pursuit of riches for their own sake. For wealth in itself was a temptation. But here asceticism was the power "which ever seeks the good but ever creates evil" what was evil in its sense was possession and its temptations. For, in conformity with the Old Testament and in analogy to the ethical valuation of good works, asceticism looked upon the pursuit of wealth as an end in itself as highly reprehensible; but the attainment of it as a fruit of labour in a calling was a sign of God's blessing. And even more important: the religious valuation of restless, continuous, systematic work in a worldly calling, a the highest means to asceticism, and at the same time the surest and most evident proof of rebirth and genuine faith, must have been the most powerful conceivable lever for the expansion of that attitude toward life which we have here called the spirit of capitalism.

When the limitation of consumption is combined with this release of acquisitive activity, the inevitable practical result is obvious: accumulation of capital through ascetic compulsion to save. The restraints which were imposed upon the consumption of wealth naturally served to increase it by making possible the productive investment of capital. How strong this influence was is not, unfortunately, susceptible o exact statistical demonstration. In New England the connection is so evident that it did not escape the eye of so discerning a historian as Doyle. But also in Holland, which was really only dominated by strict Calvinism for seven years, the greater simplicity of life in the more seriously religious circles, in combination with great wealth, led to an excessive propensity to accumulation.

That, furthermore, the tendency which has existed everywhere and at all times, being quite strong in Germany today, for middle-class fortunes to be absorbed into the nobility, was necessarily checked by the Puritan antipathy to the feudal way of life, is evident. English Mercantilist writers of the seventeenth century attributed the superiority of Dutch capital to English to the circumstance that newly acquired wealth there did not regularly seek investment in land. Also, since it is not simply a question of the purchase of land, it did not there seek to transfer itself to feudal habits of life, and thereby to remove itself from the possibility of capitalistic investment." The high esteem for agriculture as a peculiarly important branch of activity, also especially consistent with piety, which the Puritans shared, applied (for instance in Baxter) not to the landlord, but to the yeoman and farmer, in the eighteenth century not to the squire, but the rational cultivator. Through the whole of English society in the time since the seventeenth century goes the conflict between the squirearchy, the representatives of "merrie old England", and the Puritan circles of widely varying social influence. Both elements, that of an unspoiled naive joy of life, and of a strictly regulated, reserved self-control, and conventional ethical conduct are even today combined to form the English national character. Similarly, the early history of the North American Colonies is dominated by the sharp contrast of the adventurers, who wanted to set up plantations with the labour of indentured servants, and live as feudal lords, and the specifically middle-class outlook of the Puritans.

As far as the influence of the Puritan outlook extended, under all circumstances-and this is, of course, much more important than the mere encouragement of capital accumulation—it favoured the development of a rational bourgeois economic life; it was the most important, and above all the only consistent influence in the development of that life. It stood at the cradle of the modern economic man.

To be sure, these Puritanical ideals tended to give way under excessive pressure from the temptations of wealth, as the Puritans themselves knew very well. With great regularity we find the most genuine adherents of Puritanism among the classes which were rising from a lowly status, the small bourgeois and farmers, while the *beati possidentes*, even among Quakers, are often found tending to repudiate the old ideals. It was the same fate which again and again befell the predecessor of this worldly asceticism, the monastic asceticism of the Middle Ages. In the latter case, when rational economic activity had worked out its full effects by strict regulation of conduct and limitation of consumption, the wealth accumulated either succumbed directly to the nobility, as in the time before the Reformation, or monastic discipline threatened to break down, and one of the numerous reformations became necessary.

In fact the whole history of monasticism is in a certain sense the history of a continual struggle with the problem of the secularizing influence of wealth. The same is true on a grand scale of the worldly asceticism of Puritanism. The great revival of Methodism, which preceded the expansion of English industry toward the end of the eighteenth century, may well be compared with such a monastic reform. We may hence quote here a passage from John Wesley himself which might well serve as a motto for everything which has been said above. For it shows that the leaders of these ascetic movements understood the seemingly paradoxical relationships which we have here analysed perfectly well, and in the same sense that we have given them. He wrote:

"I fear, wherever riches have increased, the essence of religion has decreased in the same proportion. Therefore I do not see how it is possible, in the nature of things, for any revival of true religion to continue long. For religion must necessarily produce both industry and frugality, and these cannot but produce riches. But as riches increase, so will pride, anger, and love of the world in all its branches. How then is it possible that Methodism, that is, a religion of the heart, though it flourishes now as a green bay tree, should continue in this state? For the Methodists in every place grow diligent and frugal; consequently they increase in goods. Hence they proportionately increase in pride, in anger, in the desire of the flesh, the desire of the eyes, and the pride of life. So, although the form of religion remains, the spirit is swiftly vanishing away. Is there no way to prevent this-this continual decay of pure religion? We ought not to prevent people from being diligent and frugal; *we must exhort all Christians to gain all they can, and to save all they can; that is, in effect, to grow rich."*

There follows the advice that those who gain all they can and save all they can should also give all they can, so that they will grow in grace and lay up a treasure in heaven. It is clear that Wesley here expresses, even in detail, just what we have been trying to point out.

As Wesley here says, the full economic effect of those great religious movements, whose significance for economic development lay above all in their ascetic educative influence, generally came only after the peak of the purely religious enthusiasm was past. Then the intensity of the search for the Kingdom of God commenced gradually to pass over into sober economic virtue; the religious roots died out slowly, giving way to utilitarian worldliness. Then, as Dowden puts it, as in *Robinson Crusoe*, the isolated economic man who carries on missionary activities on the side takes the place of the lonely spiritual search for the Kingdom of Heaven of Bunyan's pilgrim, hurrying through the market-place of Vanity.

When later the principle "to make the most of both worlds" became dominant in the end, as Dowden has remarked, a good conscience simply became one of the means of enjoying a comfortable bourgeois life, as is well expressed in the German proverb about the soft pillow. What the great religious epoch of the seventeenth century bequeathed to its utilitarian successor was, however, above all an amazingly good, we may even say a pharisaically good, conscience in the acquisition of money, so long as it took place legally. Every trace of the *deplacere vix potest* has disappeared.

A specifically bourgeois economic ethic had grown up. With the consciousness of standing in the fullness of God's grace and being visibly blessed by Him, the bourgeois business man, as long as he remained within the bounds of formal correctness, as long as his moral conduct was spotless and the use to which he put his wealth was not objectionable, could follow his pecuniary interests as he would and feel that he was fulfilling a duty in doing so. The power of religious asceticism provided him in addition with sober, conscientious, and unusually industrious workmen, who clung to their work as to a life purpose willed by God.

Finally, it gave him the comforting assurance that the unequal distribution of the goods of this world was a special dispensation of Divine Providence, which in these differences, as in particular grace, pursued secret ends unknown to men. Calvin himself had made the much-quoted statement that only when the people, i.e. the mass of labourers and craftsmen, were poor did they remain obedient to God. In the Netherlands (Pieter de la Court and others), that had been secularized to the effect that the mass of men only labour when necessity forces them to do so. This formulation of a leading idea of capitalistic economy later entered into the current theories of the productivity of low wages. Here also, with the dying out of the religious root, the utilitarian interpretation crept in unnoticed, in the line of development which we have again and again observed.

Medieval ethics not only tolerated begging but actually glorified it in the mendicant orders. Even secular beggars, since they gave the person of means opportunity for good works through giving alms, were sometimes considered an estate and treated as such. Even the Anglican social ethic of the Stuarts was very close to this attitude. It remained for Puritan Asceticism to take part in the severe English Poor Relief Legislation which fundamentally changed the situation. And it could do that because the Protestant sects and the strict Puritan communities actually did not know any begging in their own midst.

On the other hand, seen from the side of the workers, the Zinzendorf branch of Pietism, for instance, glorified the loyal worker who did not seek acquisition, but lived according to the apostolic model, and was thus endowed with the *charisma* of the disciples. Similar ideas had originally been prevalent among the Baptists

Now naturally the whole ascetic literature of almost all denominations is saturated with the idea that faithful labour, even at low wages, on the part of those whom, life offers no other opportunities, is highly pleasing to God. In this respect Protestant Asceticism added in itself nothing new. But it not only deepened this idea most powerfully, it also created the force which was alone decisive for its effectiveness: the psychological sanction of it through the conception of this labour as a calling, as the best, often in the last analysis the only means of attaining certainty of grace. And on the other hand it legalized the exploitation of this specific willingness to work, in that it also interpreted the employer's business activity as a calling. It is obvious how powerfully the exclusive search for the Kingdom of God only through the fulfillment of duty in the calling, and the strict asceticism which Church discipline naturally imposed, especially on the propertyless classes, was bound to affect the productivity of labour in the capitalistic sense of the word. The treatment of labour as a calling became as characteristic of the modern worker as the corresponding attitude toward acquisition of the business man. It was a perception of this situation, new at his time, which caused so able an observer as Sir William Petty to attribute the economic power of Holland in the seventeenth century to the fact that the very numerous dissenters in that country (Calvinists and Baptists) "are for the most

part thinking, sober men, and such as believe that Labour and Industry is their duty towards God".

Calvinism opposed organic social organization in
the fiscal-monopolistic form which it assumed in Anglicanism under the Stuarts, especially in the conceptions
of Laud, this alliance of Church and State with the monopolists on the basis of a Christian, social ethical foundation. Its leaders were universally among the most passionate opponents of this type of politically privileged
commercial, putting-out, and colonial capitalism. Over
against it they placed the individualistic motives of rational legal acquisition by virtue of one's own ability
and initiative. And, while the politically privileged mo-
nopoly industries in England all disappeared in short
order, this attitude played a large and decisive part in
the development of the industries which grew up in
spite of and against the authority of the State. The Puritans (Prynne, Parker) repudiated all connection with
the large-scale capitalistic courtiers and projectors as an
ethically suspicious class. On the other hand, they took
pride in their own superior middle-class business morality, which formed the true reason for the persecutions
to which they were subjected on the part of those circles. Defoe proposed to win the battle against dissent by
boycotting bank credit and withdrawing deposits. The
difference of the two types of capitalistic attitude went
to a very large extent hand in hand with religious differences. The opponents of the Nonconformists, even in the
eighteenth century, again and again ridiculed them for
personifying the spirit of shopkeepers, and for having
ruined the ideals of old England. Here also lay the difference of the Puritan economic ethic from the Jewish; and
contemporaries (Prynne) knew well that the former and
not the latter was the bourgeois capitalistic ethic.

One of the fundamental elements of the spirit of
modern capitalism, and not only of that but of all modern culture: rational conduct on the basis of the idea of
the calling, was born--that is what this discussion has
sought to demonstrate-from the spirit of Christian asceticism. One has only to reread the passage from Franklin,

quoted at the beginning of this essay, in order to see that the essential elements of the attitude which was there called the spirit of capitalism are the same as what we have just shown to be the content of the Puritan worldly asceticism, only without the religious basis, which by Franklin's time bad died away. The idea that modern labour has an ascetic character is of course not new. Limitation to specialized work, with a renunciation of the Faustian universality of man which it involves, is a condition of any valuable work in the modern world; hence deeds and renunciation inevitably condition each other today. This fundamentally ascetic trait of middle-class life, if it attempts to be a way of life at all, and not simply the absence of any, was what Goethe wanted to teach, at the height of his wisdom, in the *Wanderjahren*, and in the end which he gave to the life of his *Faust*. For him the realization meant a renunciation, a departure from an age of full and beautiful humanity, which can no more be repeated in the course of our cultural development than can the flower of the Athenian culture of antiquity.

The Puritan wanted to work in a calling; we are forced to do so. For when asceticism was carried out of monastic cells into everyday life, and began to dominate worldly morality, it did its part in building the tremendous cosmos of the modern economic order. This order is now bound to the technical and economic conditions of machine production which today determine the lives of all the individuals who are born into this mechanism, not only those directly concerned with economic acquisition, with irresistible force. Perhaps it will so determine them until the last ton of fossilized coal is burnt. In Baxter's view tile care for external goods should only lie on the shoulders of the "saint like a light cloak, which can be thrown aside at any moment". But fate decreed that the cloak should become an iron cage.

Since asceticism undertook to remodel the world and to work out its ideals in the world, material goods have gained an increasing and finally an inexorable power over the lives of men as at no previous period in history. Today the spirit of religious asceticism — whether finally, who knows?—has escaped from the cage. But victorious capitalism, since it rests on mechanical foundations, needs its support no longer. The rosy blush of its laughing heir, the Enlightenment, seems also to be irretrievably fading, and the idea of duty in one's calling prowls about in our lives like the ghost of dead religious beliefs. Where the fulfillment of the calling cannot directly be related to the highest spiritual and cultural values, or when, on the other hand, it need not be felt simply as economic compulsion, the individual generally abandons the attempt to justify it at all. In the field of its highest development, in the United States, the pursuit of wealth, stripped of its religious and ethical meaning, tends to become associated with purely mundane passions, which often actually give it the character of sport.

No one knows who will live in this cage in the future, or whether at the end of this tremendous development, entirely new prophets will arise, or there will be a great rebirth of old ideas and ideals, or, if neither, mechanized petrification, embellished with a sort of convulsive self-importance. For of the fast stage of this cultural development, it might well be truly said: "Specialists without spirit, sensualists without heart; this nullity imagines that it has attained a level of civilization never before achieved."

But this brings us to the world of judgments o value and of faith, with which this purely historical discussion need not be burdened. The next task would be rather to show the significance of ascetic rationalism which has only been touched in the foregoing sketch for the content of practical social ethics, thus for the types of organization and the functions of social groups from the conventicle to the State. Then its relations to humanistic rationalism, its ideals of life and cultural influence; further to the development of philosophical and scientific empiricism, to technical development and to spiritual ideals would have to be analysed. Then its historical development from the medieval beginnings of worldly asceticism to its dissolution into pure utilitarianism would have to be traced out through all the areas of ascetic re-

ligion. Only then could the quantitative cultural significance of ascetic Protestantism in its relation to the other
plastic elements of modern culture be estimated.

Here we have only attempted to trace the fact and
the direction of its influence to their motives in one,
though a very important point. But it would also further be necessary to investigate how Protestant Asceticism was in turn influenced in its development and its
character by the totality of social conditions, especially
economic. The modern man is in general, even with the
best will, unable to give religious ideas a significance for
culture and national character which they deserve. But
it is, of course, not my aim to substitute for a one-sided
materialistic an equally one sided spiritualistic causal
interpretation of culture and of history. Each is equally
possible, but each, if it does not serve as the preparation,
but as the conclusion of an investigation, accomplish
equally little in the interest of historical truth.

Made in the USA
Middletown, DE
27 October 2023

41510808R00083